A Personal Photographic Journey

of
Karl Tani

Cover photo by Karl Tani,
India 2009

About the Author

Born in Boyle Heights, southeast of downtown Los Angeles, Karl Tani spent 4 years at two WWII internment camps where, at the age of 3, he showed his interest in art. The family moved back to L.A. then to Mar Vista, part of a segregated red-line area. He received his Bachelor of Arts degree in Design from UCLA. His career began as a graphic designer at Gould and Associates, a package design studio in Beverly Hills. As a 2 1/2 year graphic associate with Alexander Girard in Santa Fe, N.M., he was involved with many projects including the redesign of Braniff Airlines. Within his 10 years with Hood Hope and Associates in Tulsa, OK, he became a vice president executive art director. Upon his return to Southern California, he designed for San Diego art studios and advertising agencies. In a move to Orange County he was the creative director of his own studio giving him the opportunity as an adjunct instructor in Graphic Design and Typography for 15 years at Santa Ana College. The numerous stops gave him extensive experience in all phases of graphic design: logos, brochures, advertising, signage, editorial and book design, traditional hand skills of illustration, hand lettering, calligraphy, ceramics, photography and giving back as a teacher from a wonderful career.

Much of his career required photography as an essential part of the communication process, art directing professional photographers as well as observing their technical skills. UCLA began Karl's interest in photography and in retirement a wonderful hobby. He has a very eclectic eye, resulting in a diverse collection of images, many taken on frequent walks in neighborhoods and on his travels, often on tours capturing images on the fly with no consistent context. Reviewing his accumulation of photos resulted in self-published books on *Windows*, followed by *Flowers*, *Hearts* and unpublished books on *Shadows* and on *Reflections*. He has a soon-to-be published book titled *PhotoUnrealism*.

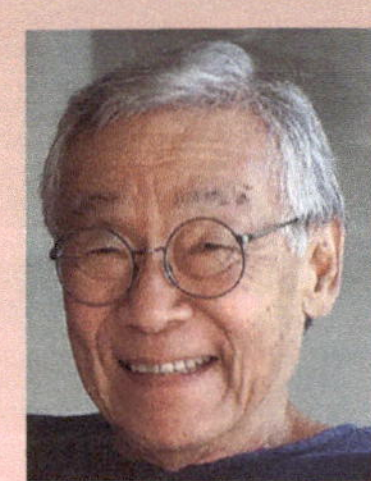

A Personal Photographic Journey

of Karl Tani

Dedicated to my incredible parents
Ruth Fusako and Fred Yutaka Tani
for their life long encouragement.

The incredible technology of cellphones has provided all of us with the ability to be instant photographers. Digital imagery allows for limitless photos without the restrictions of film, negative processing costs, and outside prints.

Family, groups, and individual photo ops are common, and the hitherto selfies taken with a landmark in the background verify oneself at a travel destination.

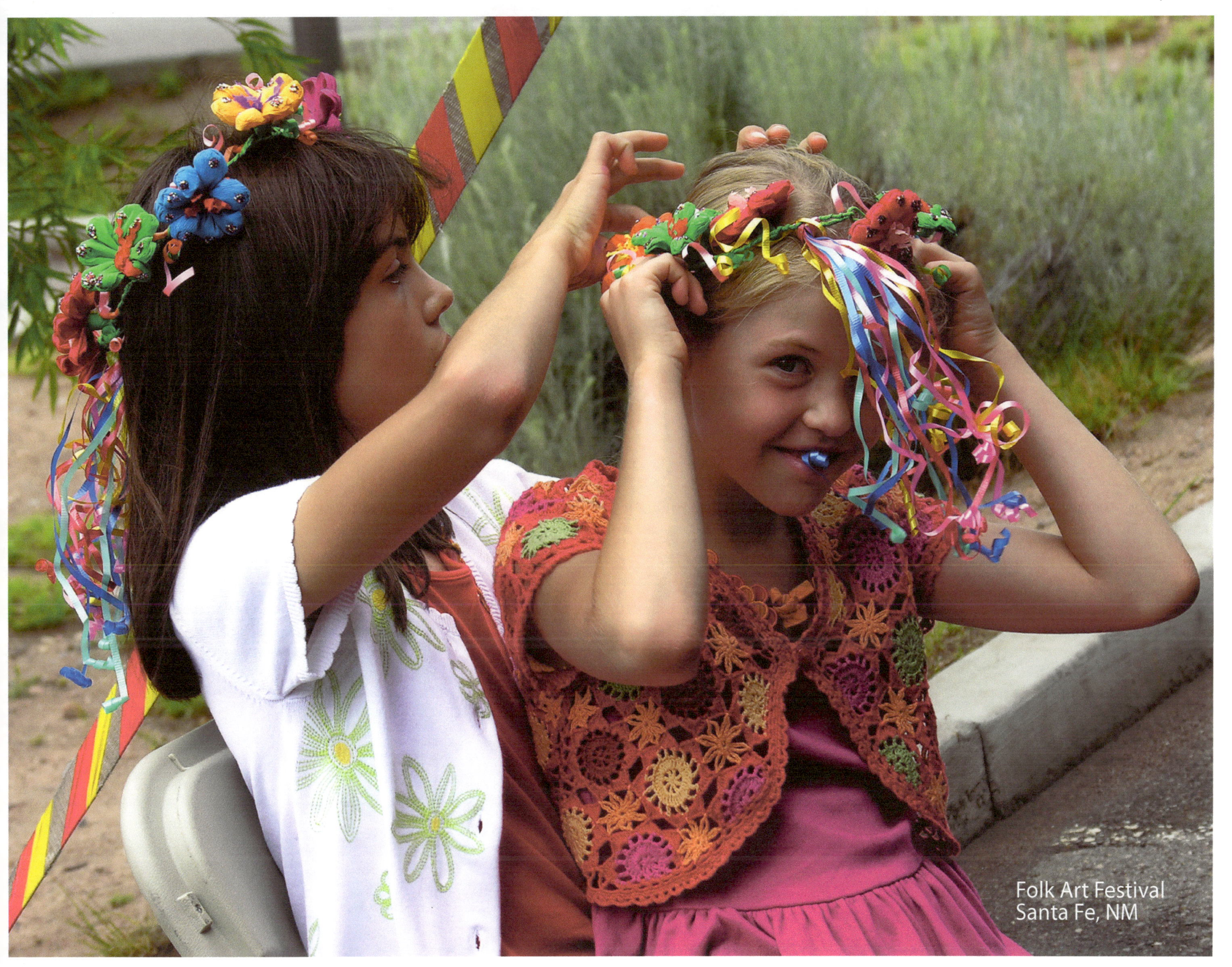

Folk Art Festival
Santa Fe, NM

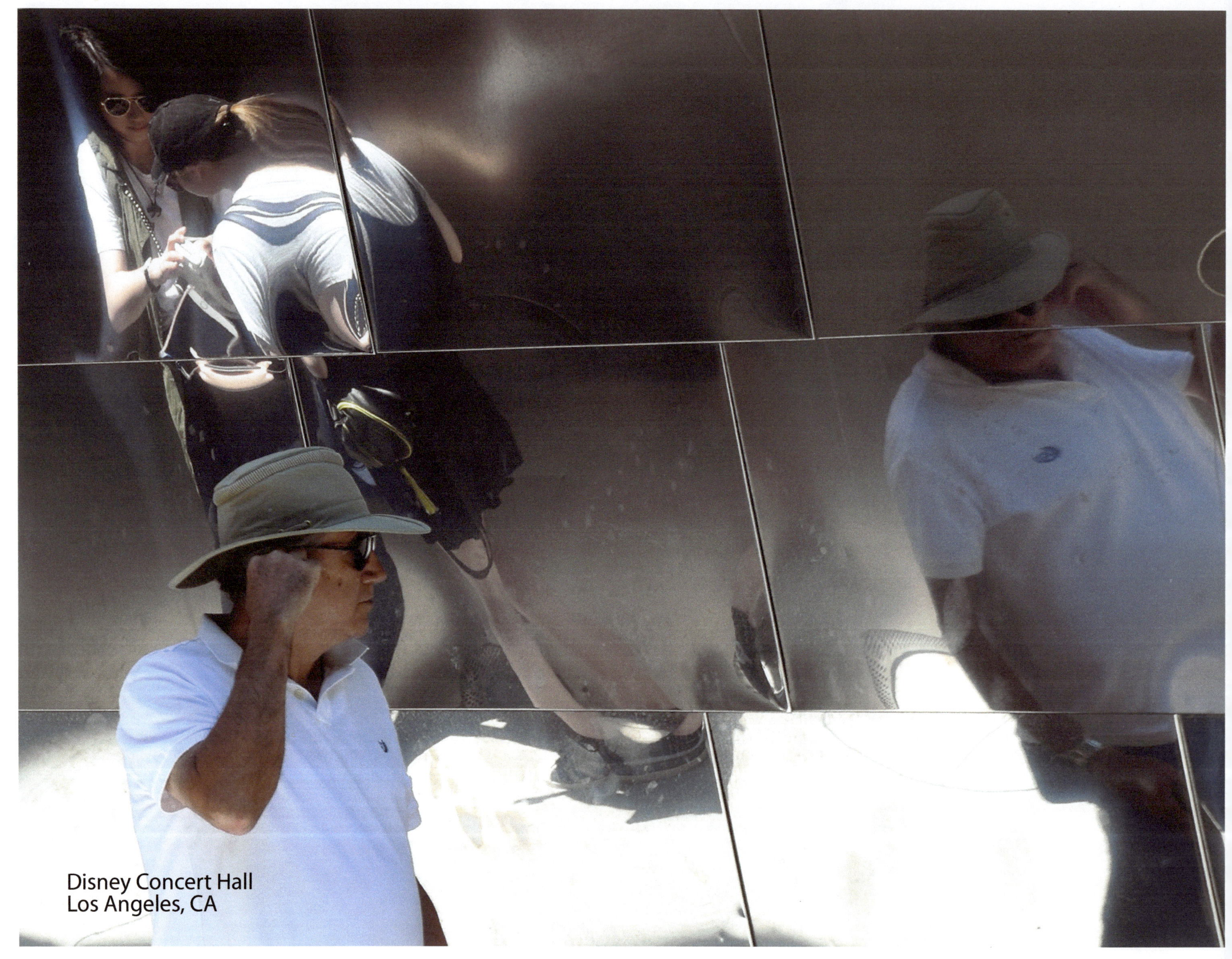

Disney Concert Hall
Los Angeles, CA

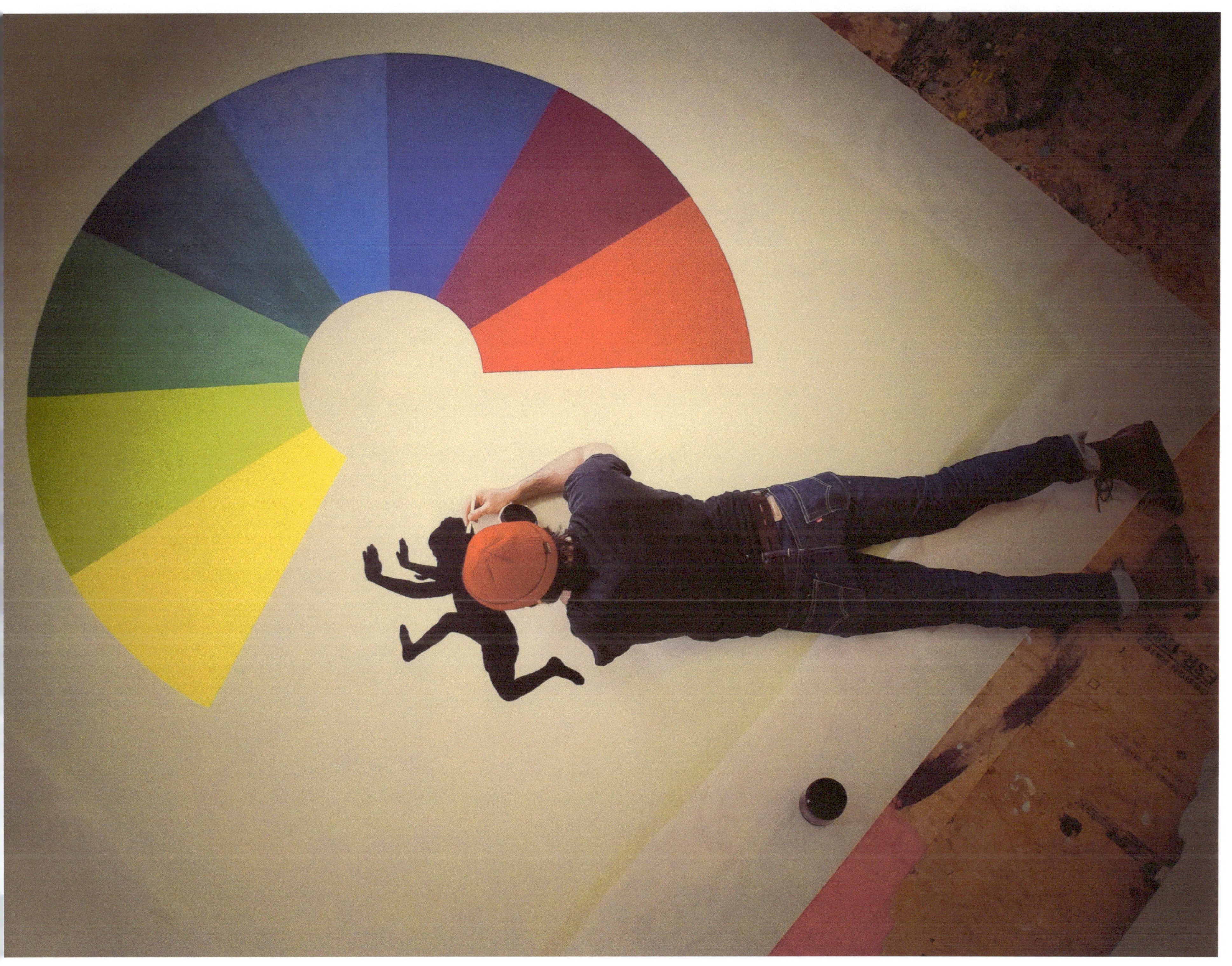

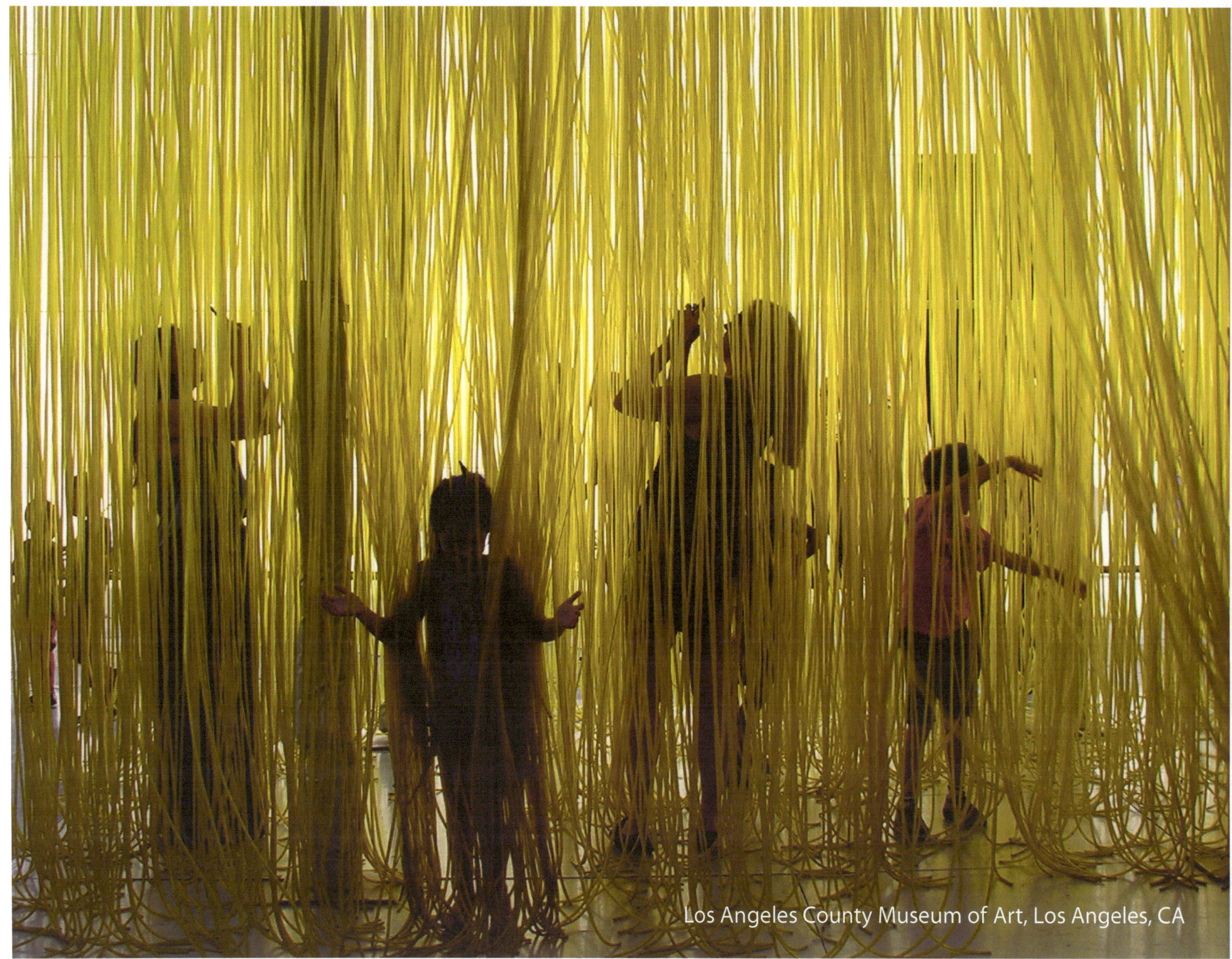

Los Angeles County Museum of Art, Los Angeles, CA

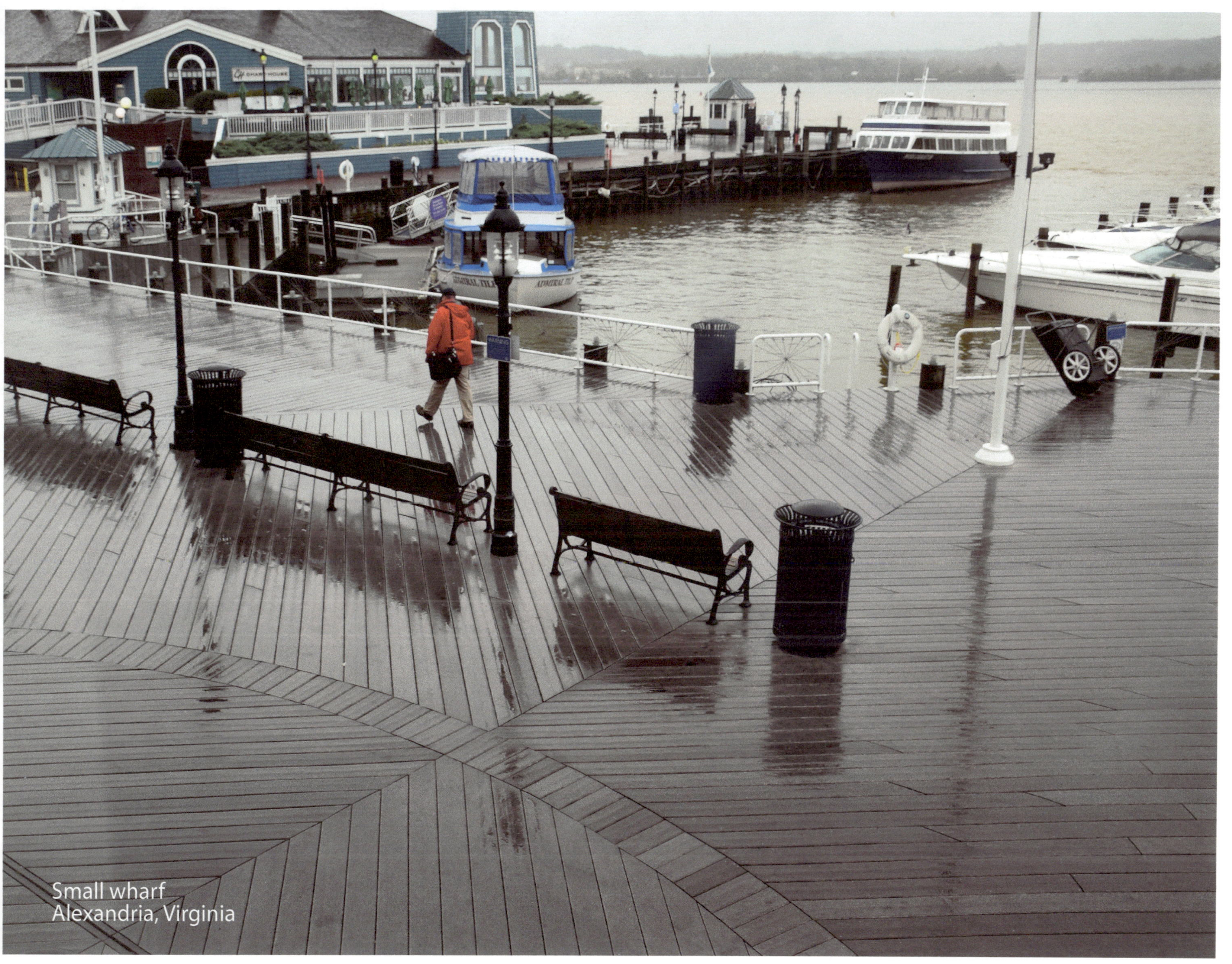

Small wharf
Alexandria, Virginia

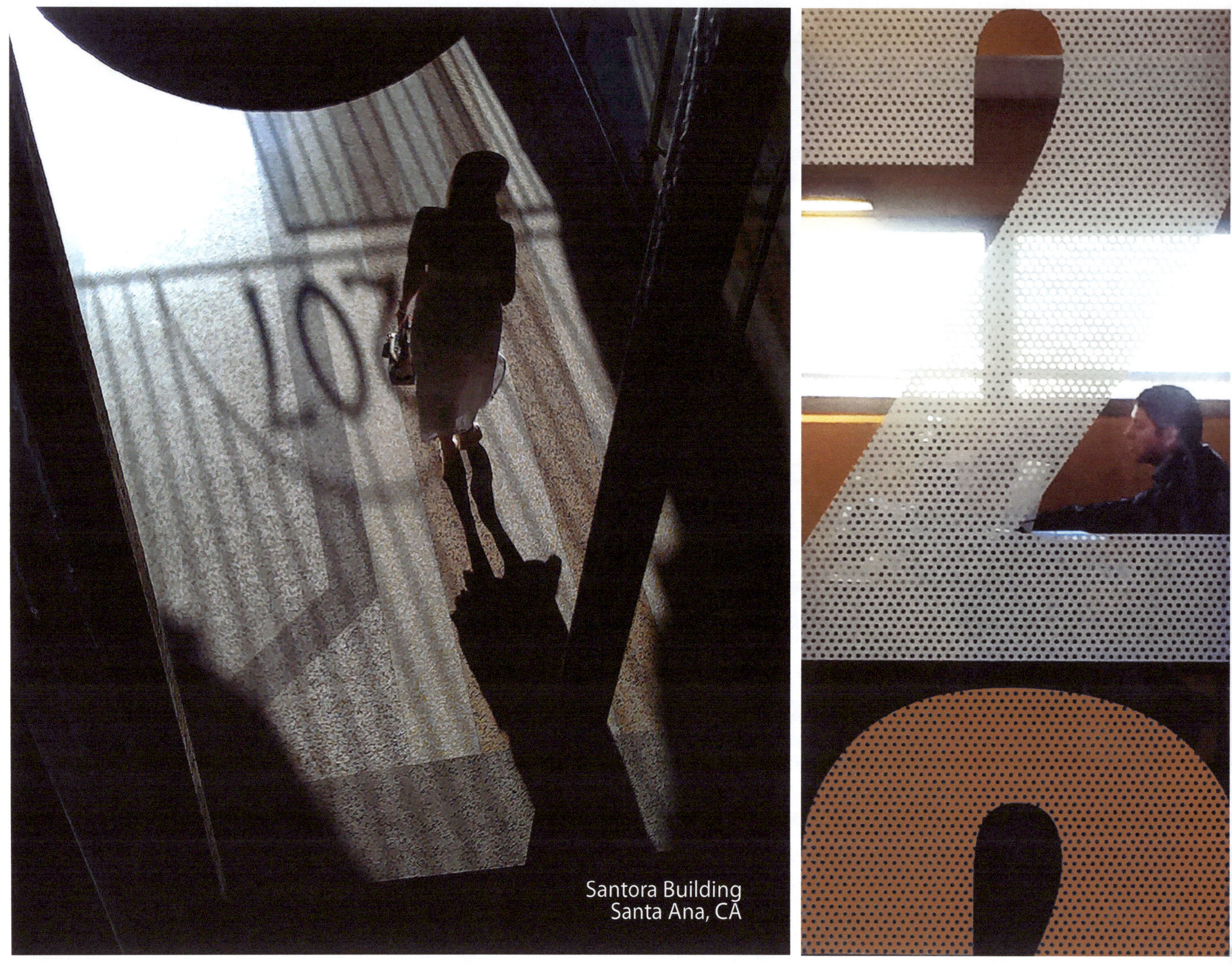
Santora Building
Santa Ana, CA

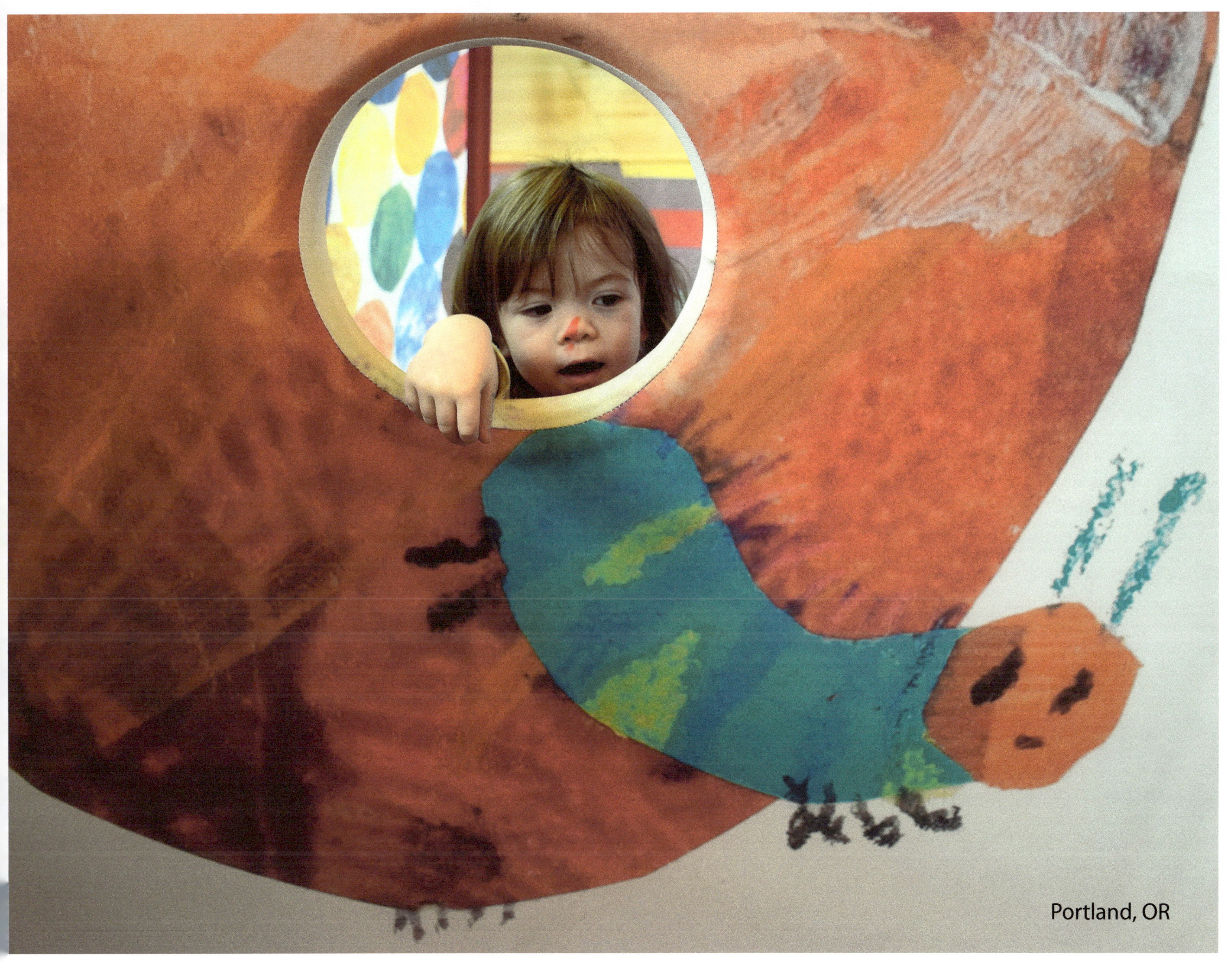

Portland, OR

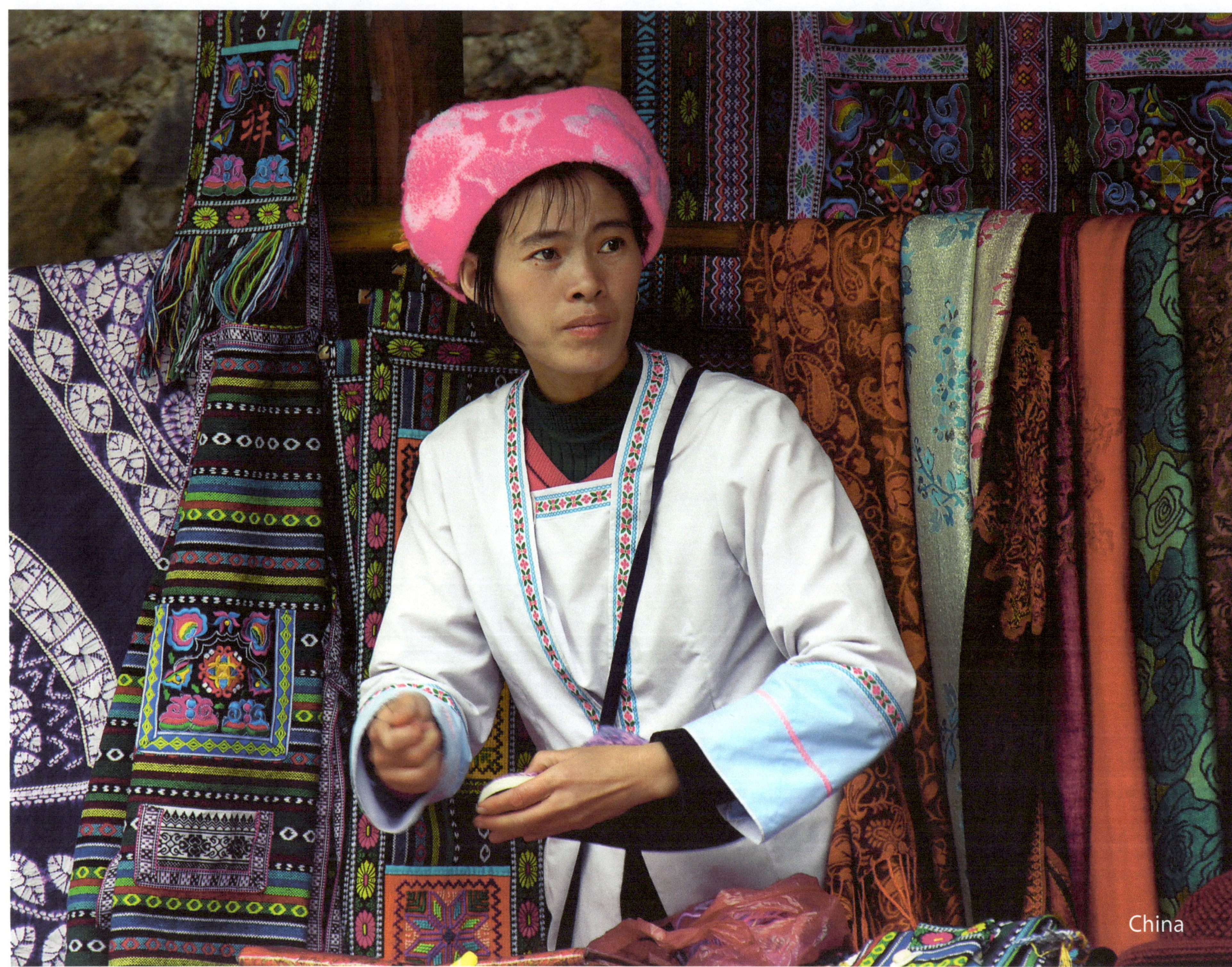
China

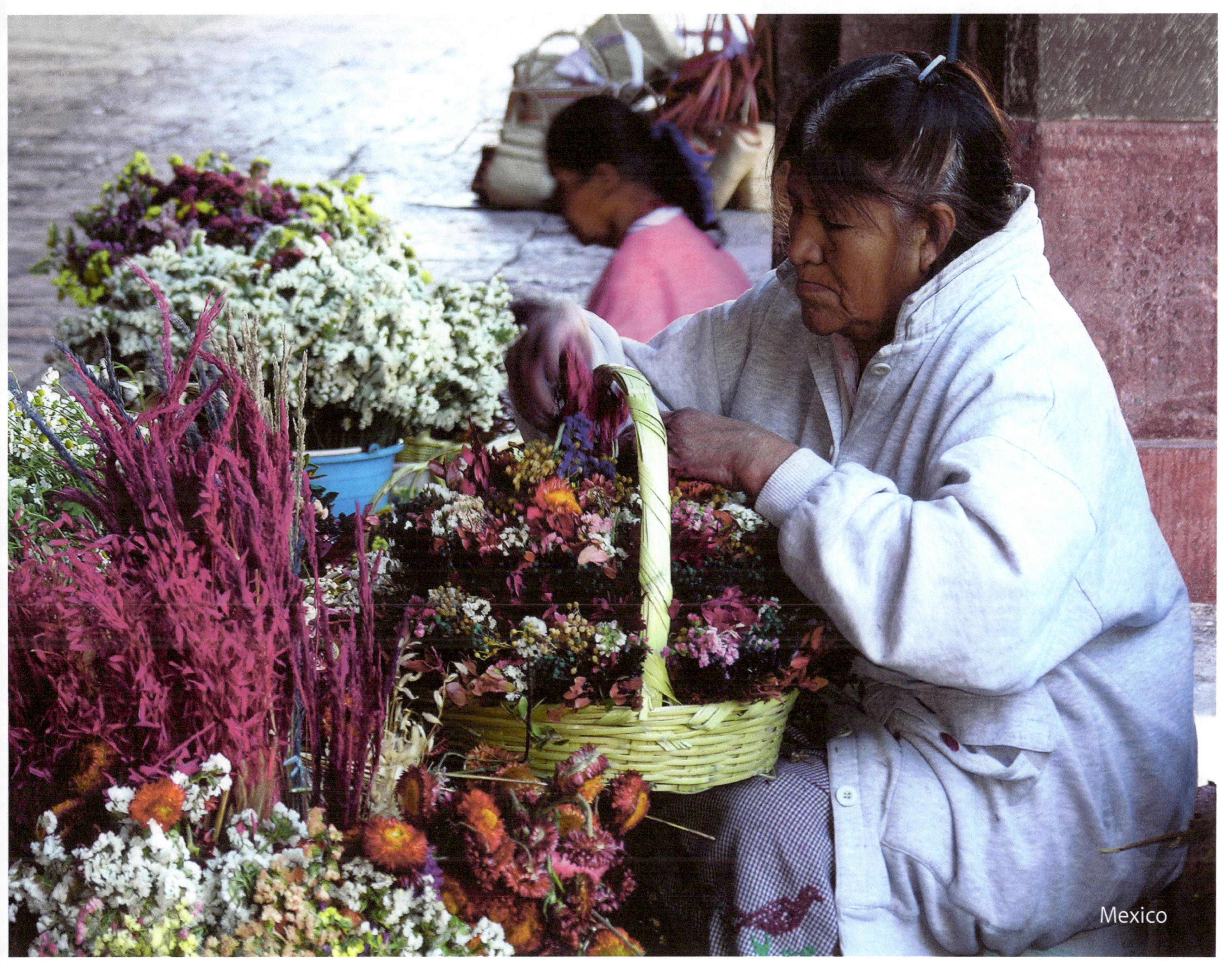
Mexico

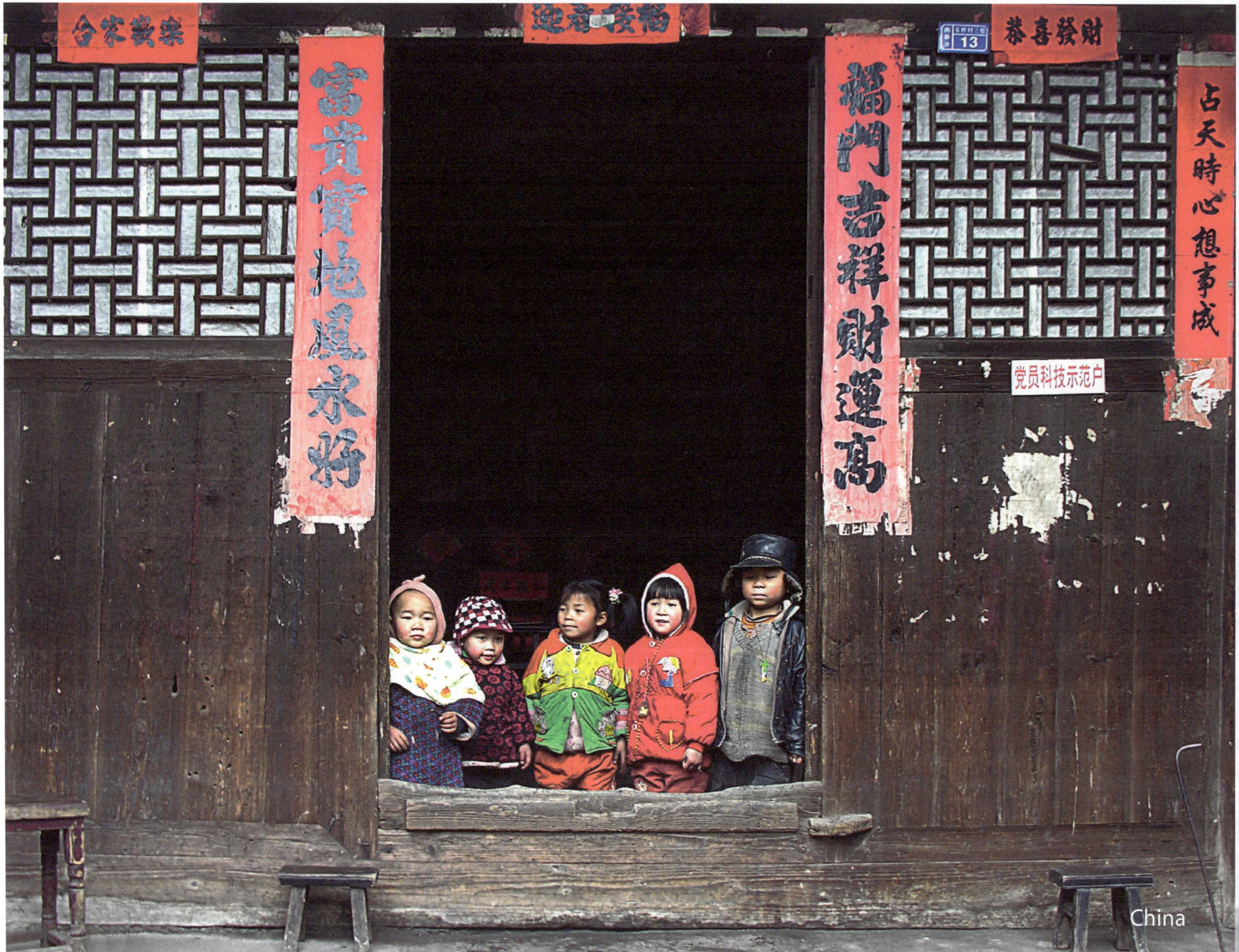

China

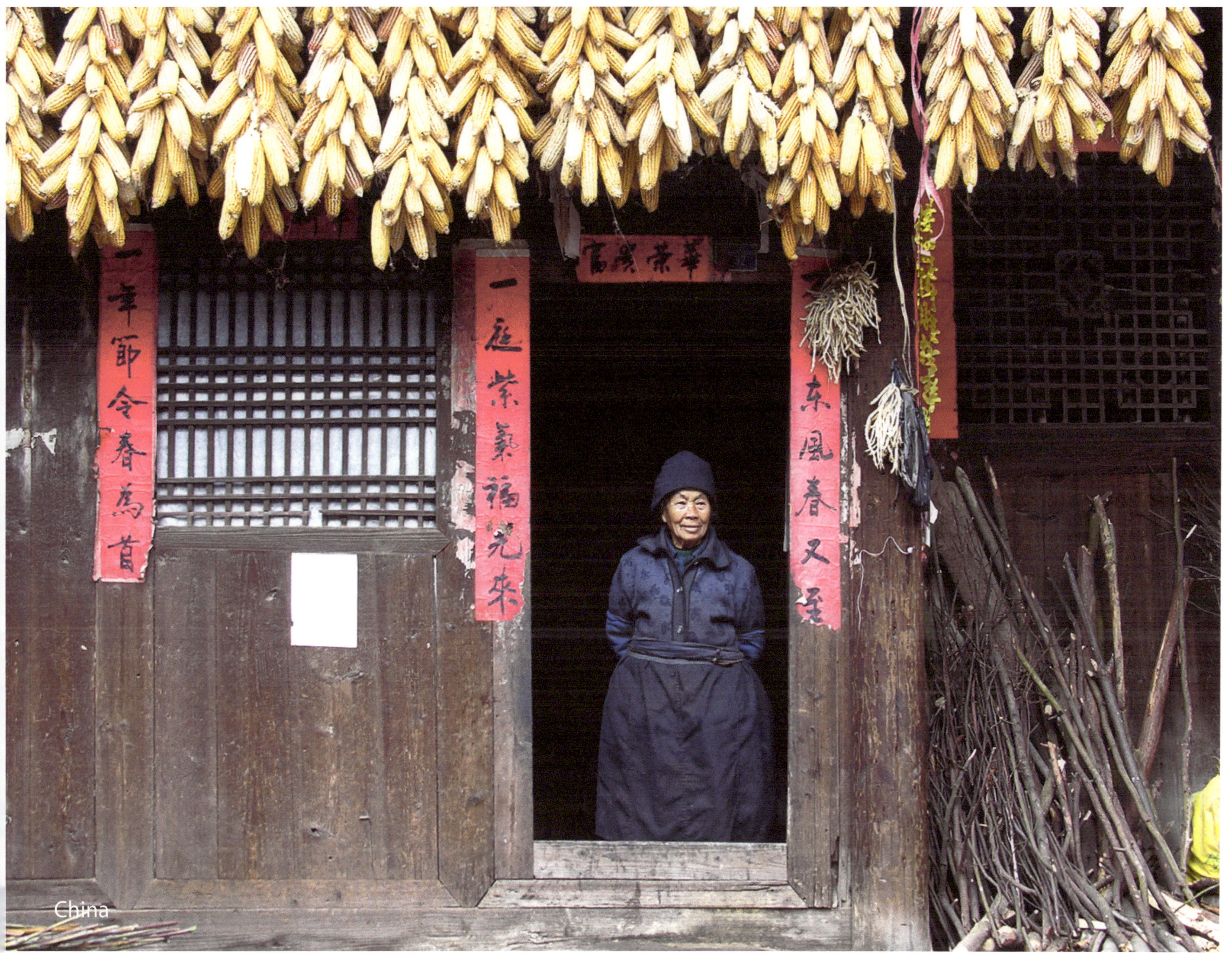

華堂集瑞
一年節令春為首
一庭紫氣福光來
東風春又至
China

Look and think
before opening the shutter.
The heart and mind
are the true lens of the camera.

- Yousuf Karsh

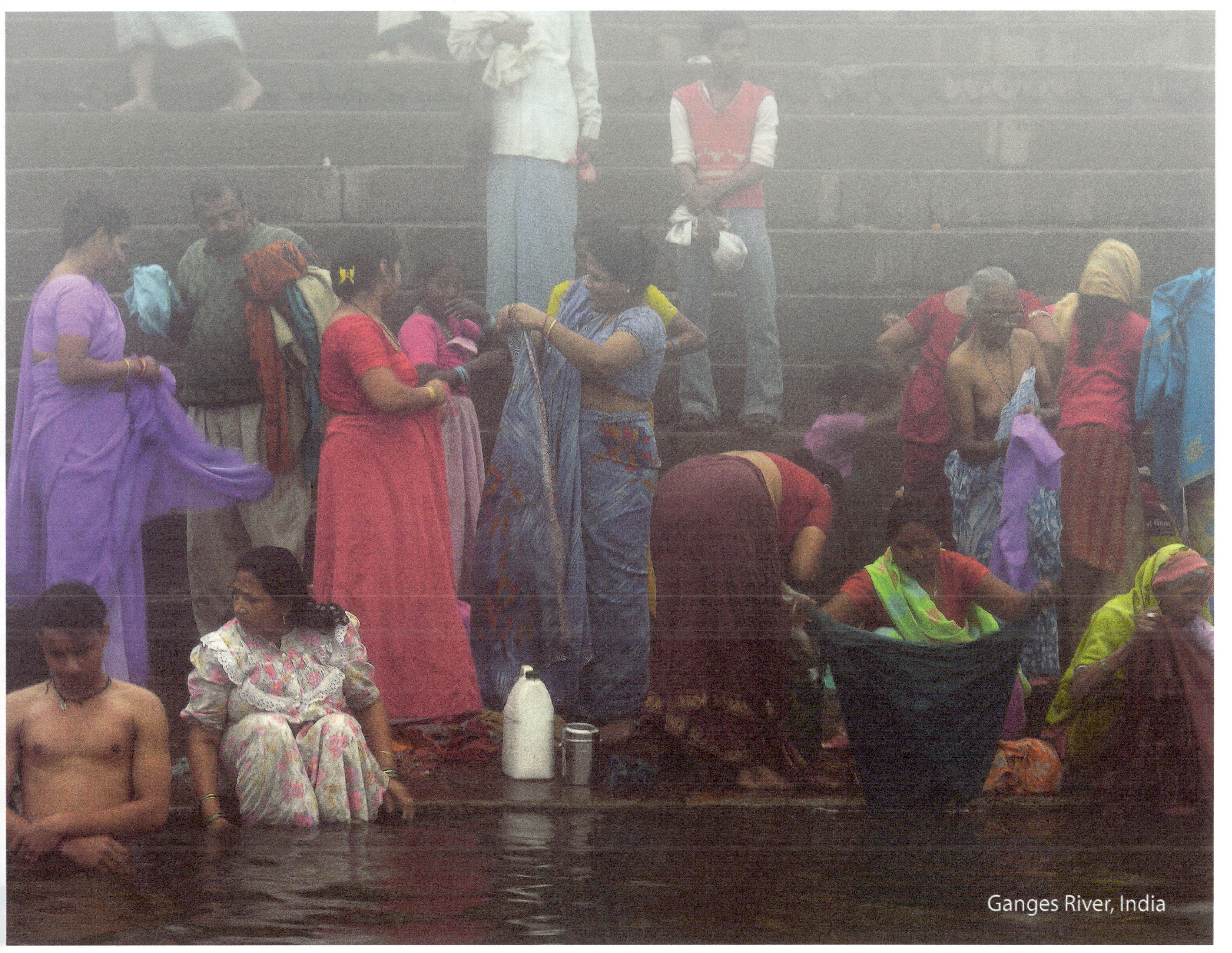
Ganges River, India

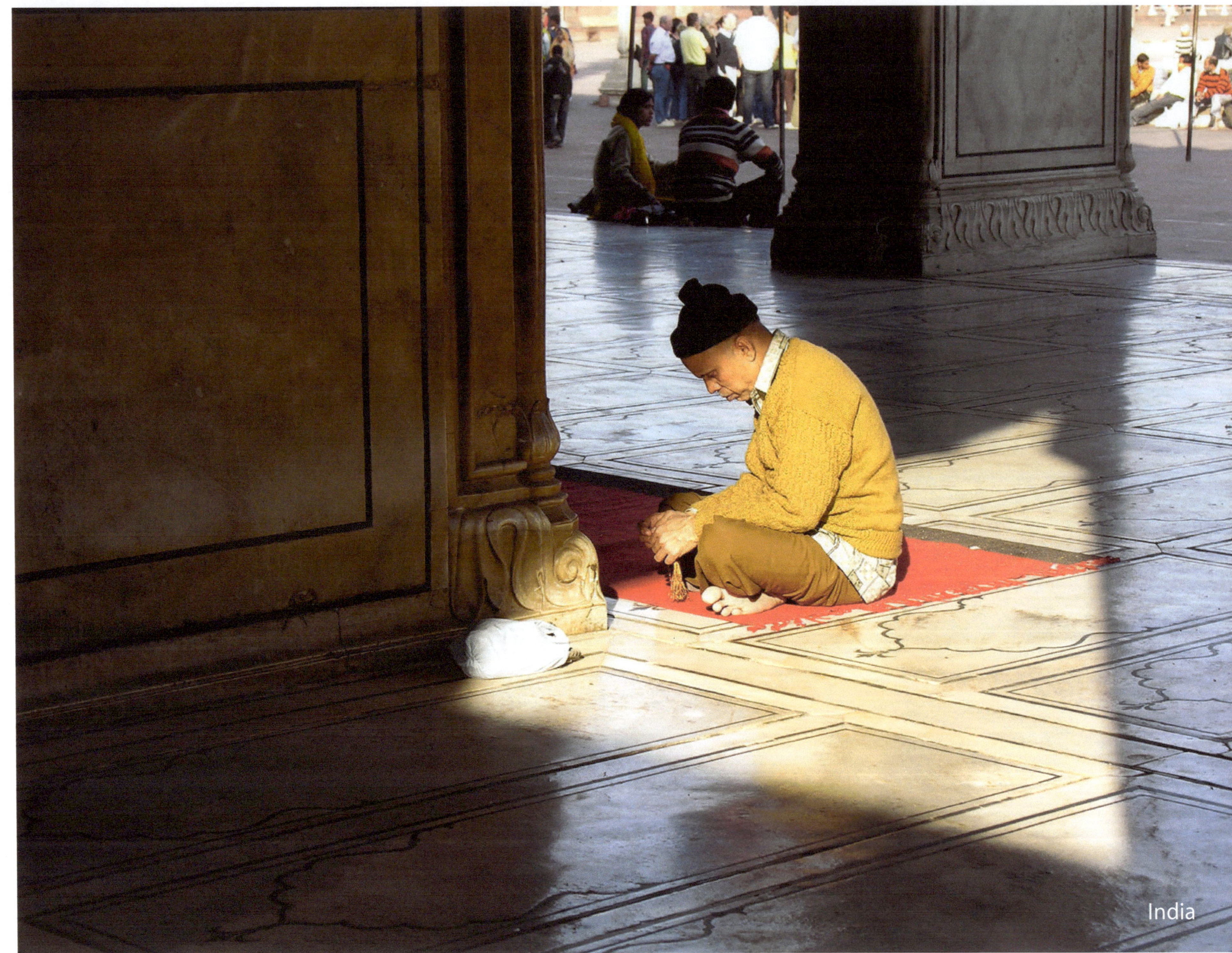

India

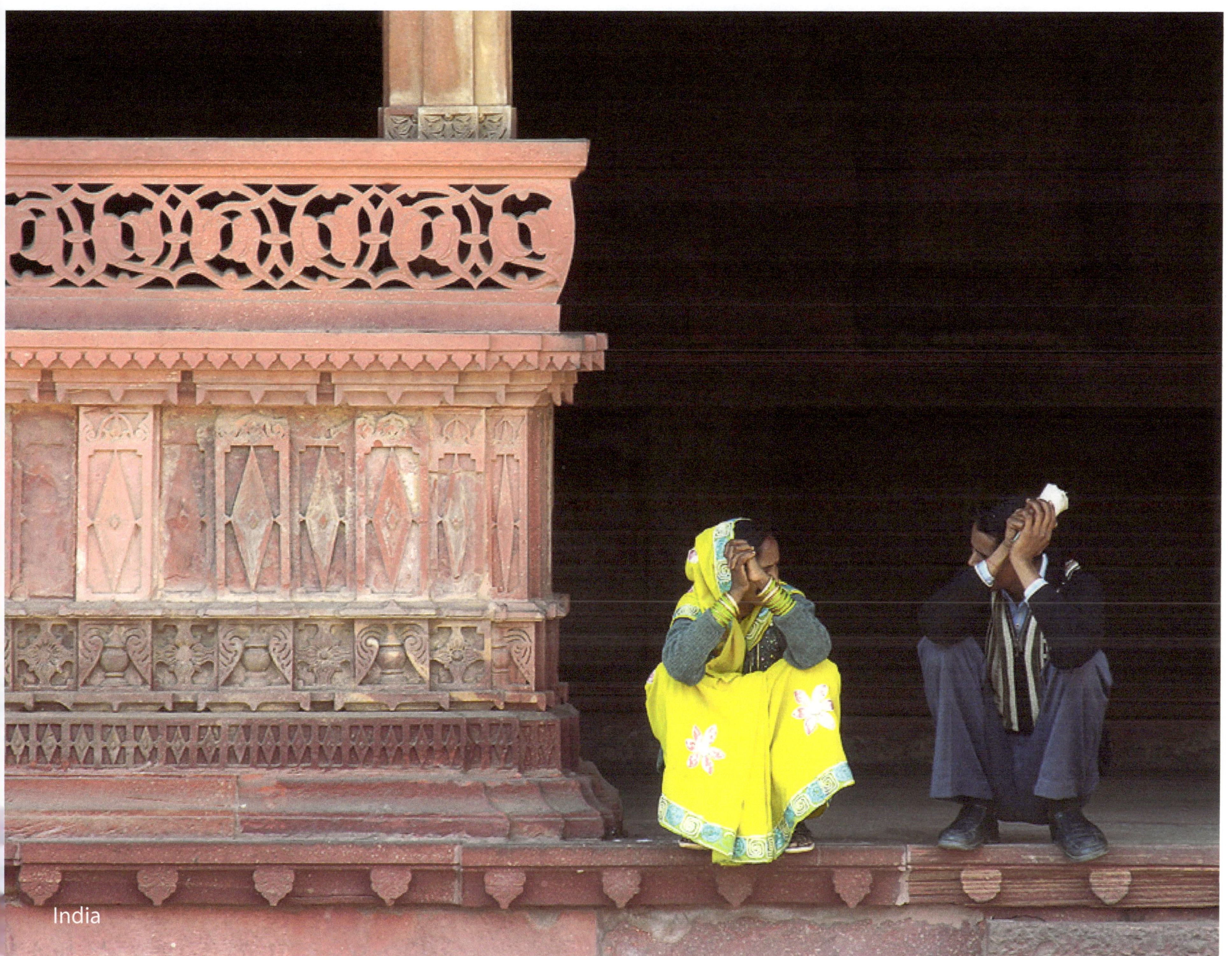
India

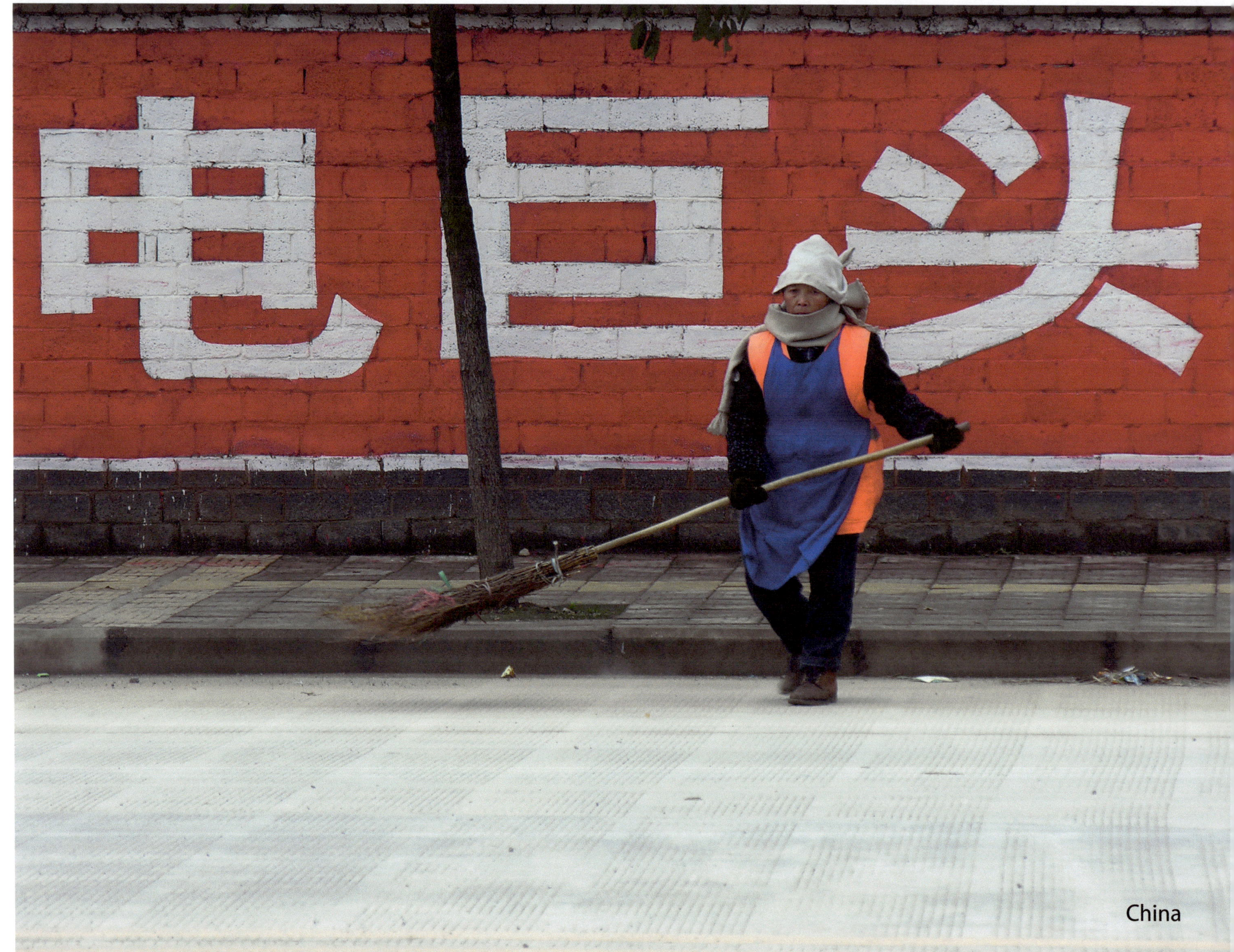

China

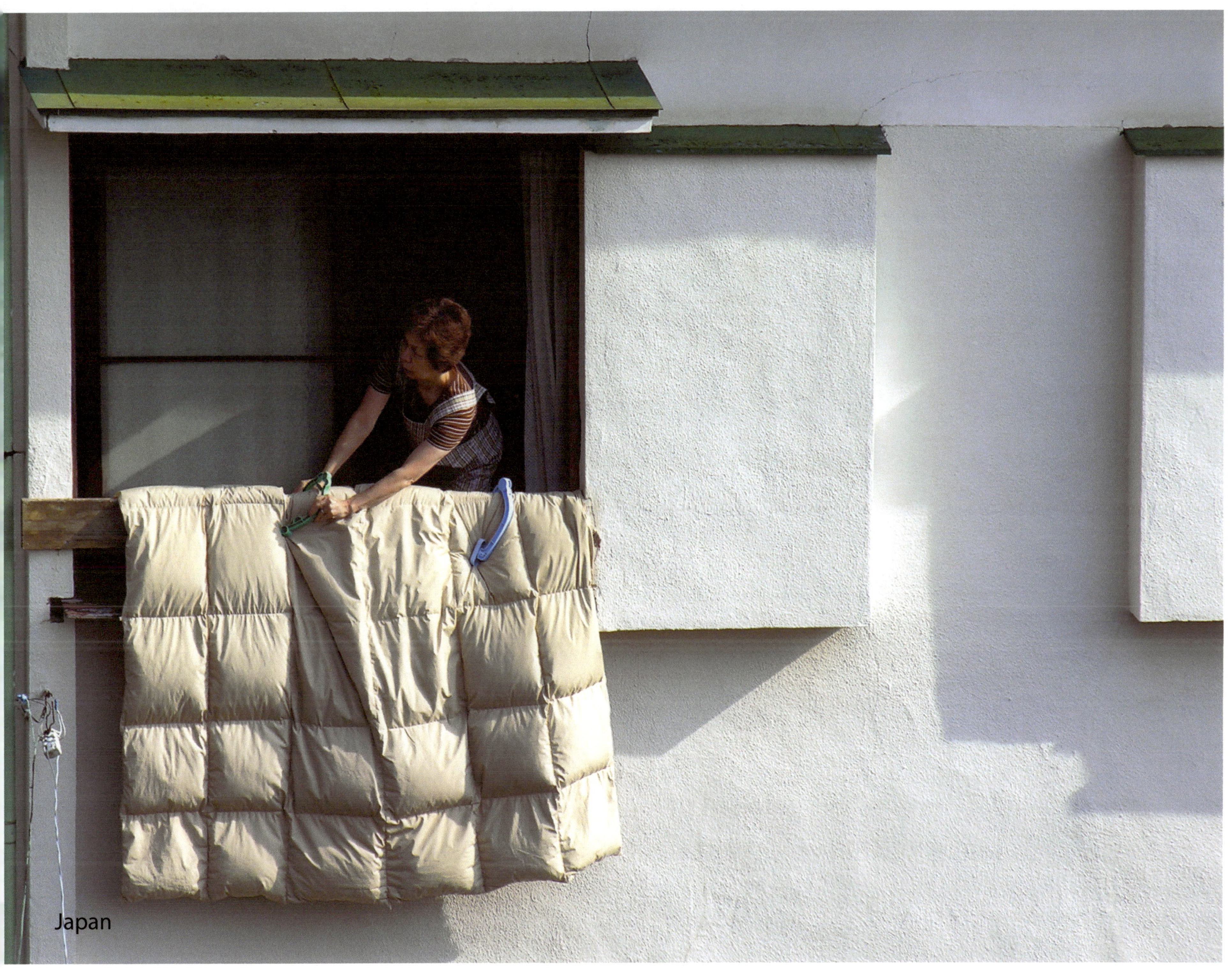

Japan

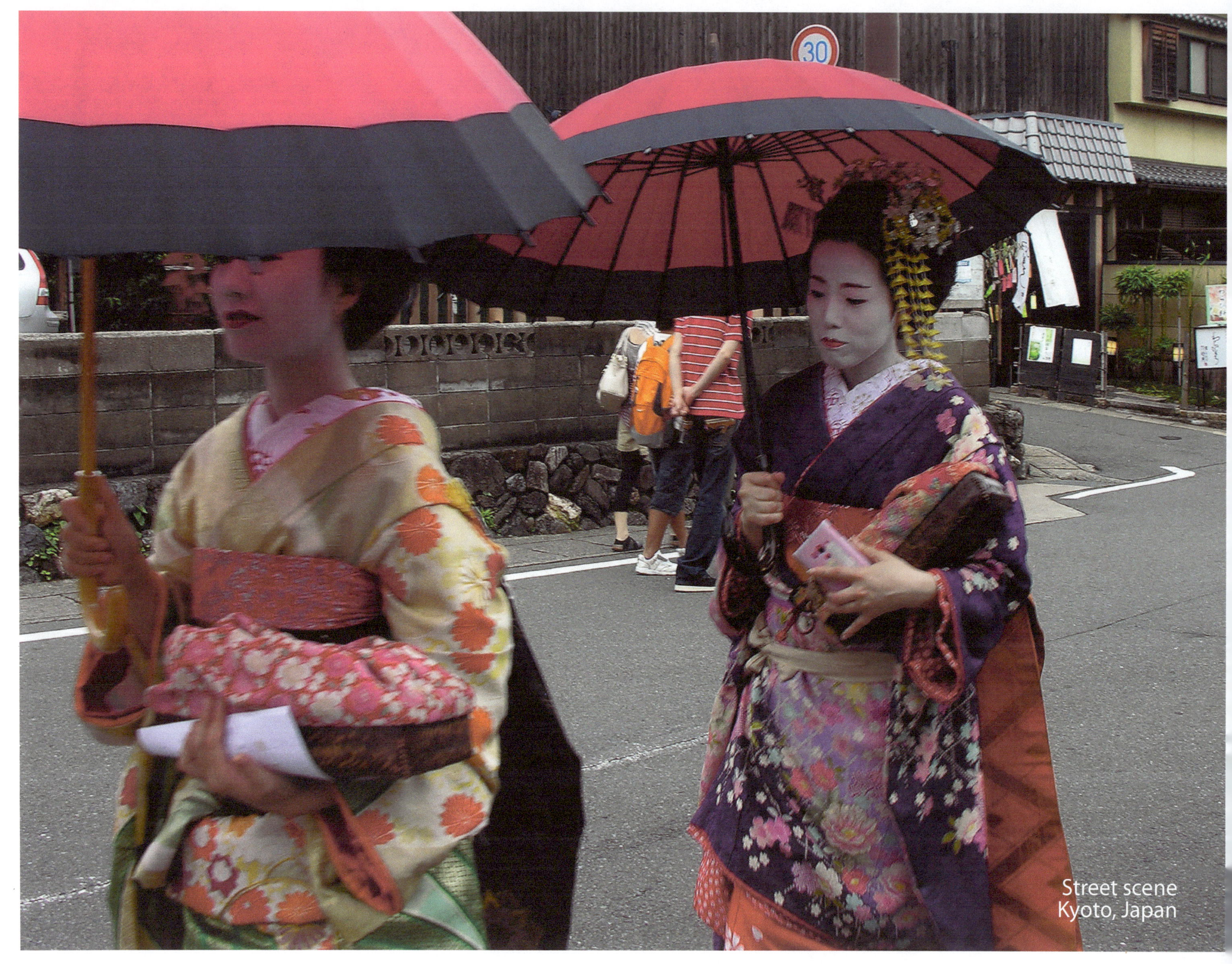
Street scene
Kyoto, Japan

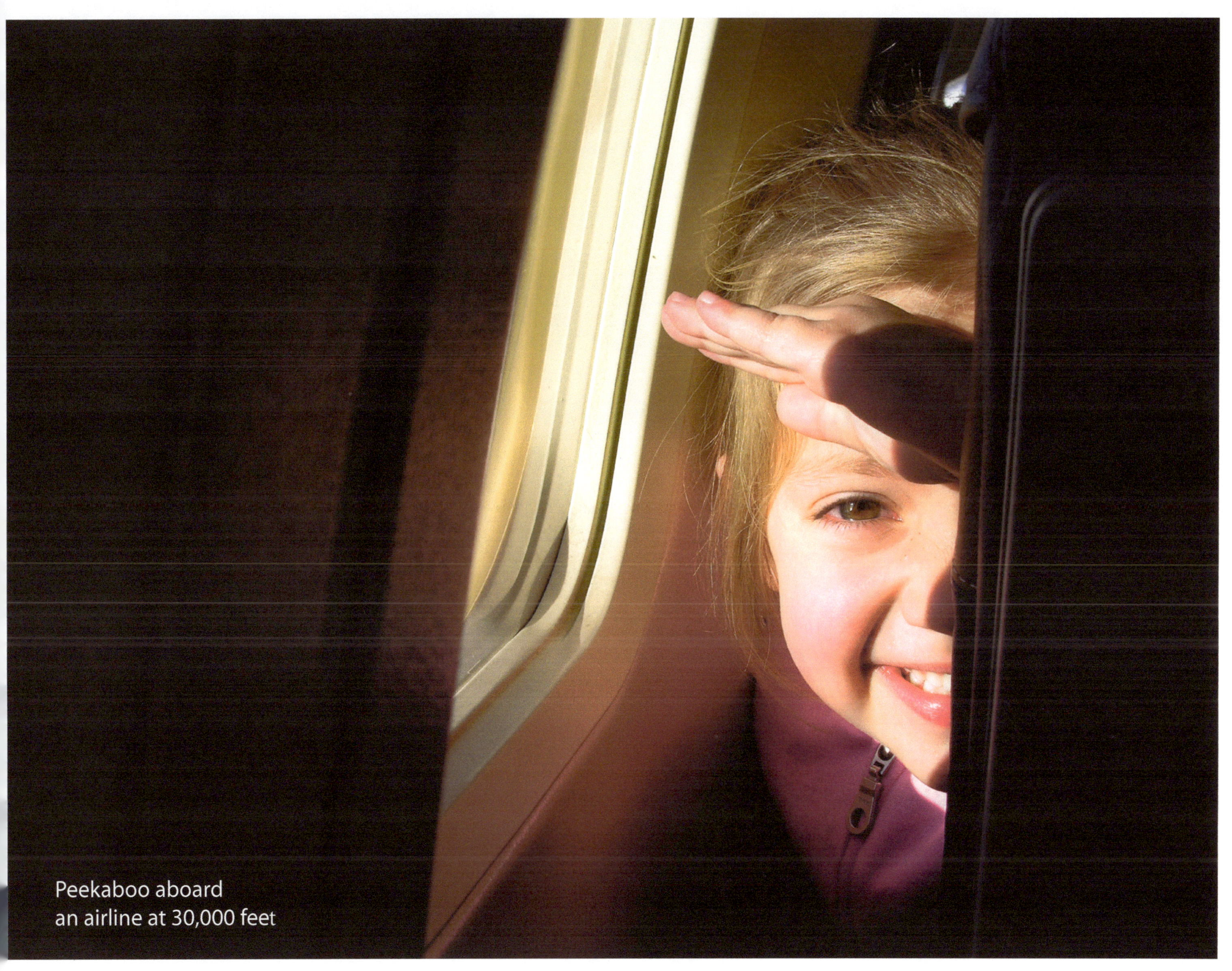
Peekaboo aboard
an airline at 30,000 feet

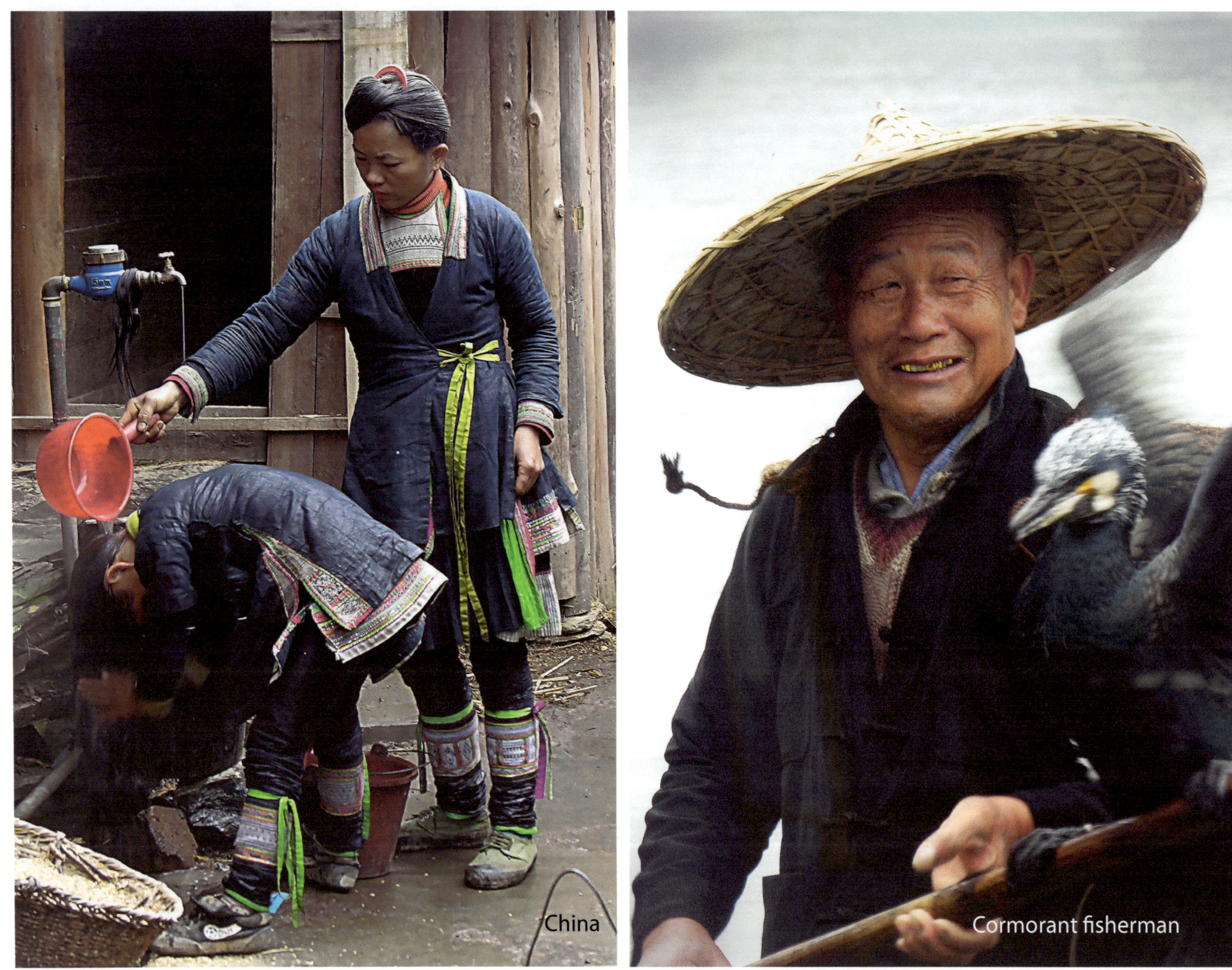

China
Cormorant fisherman

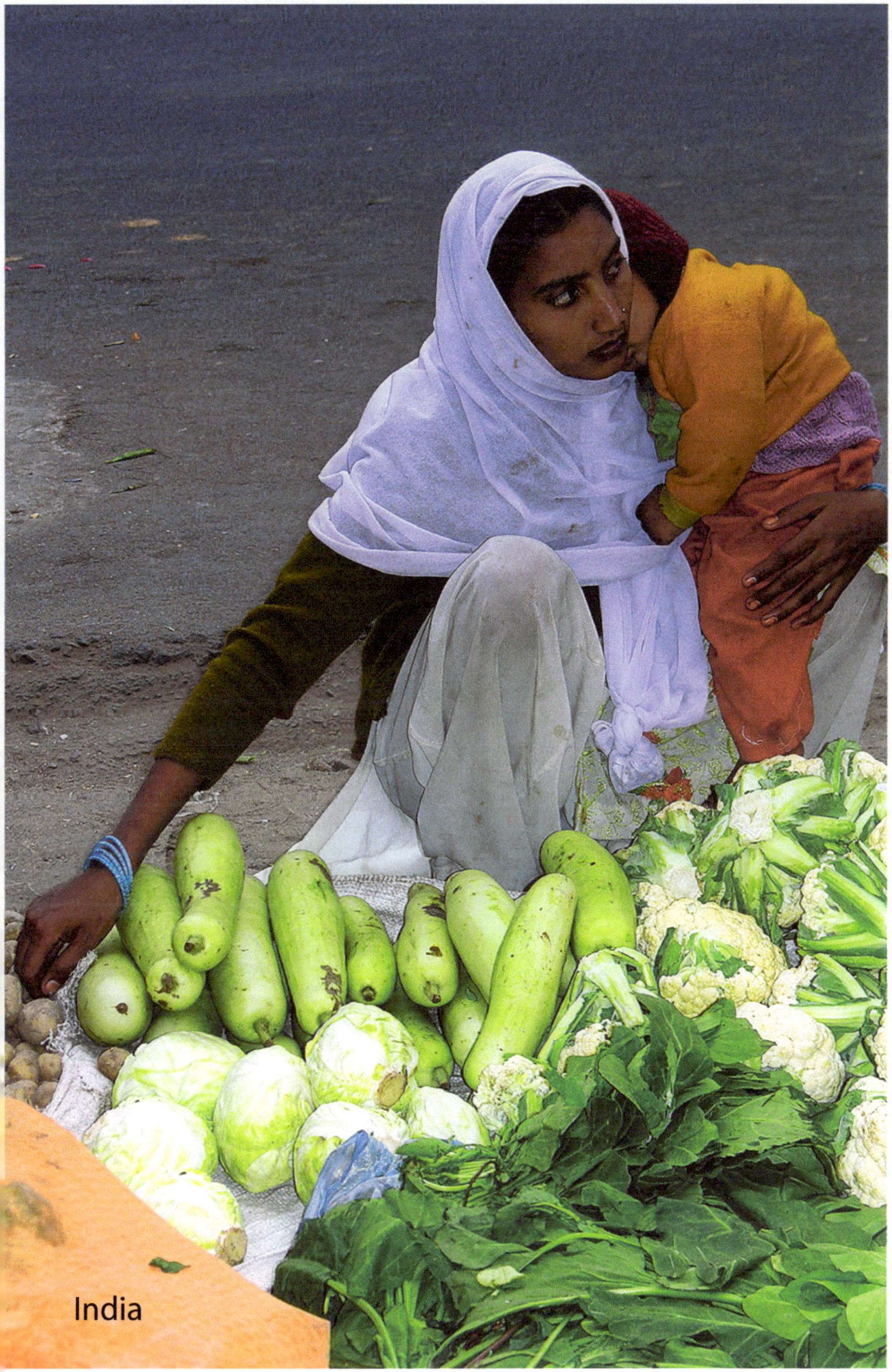

India

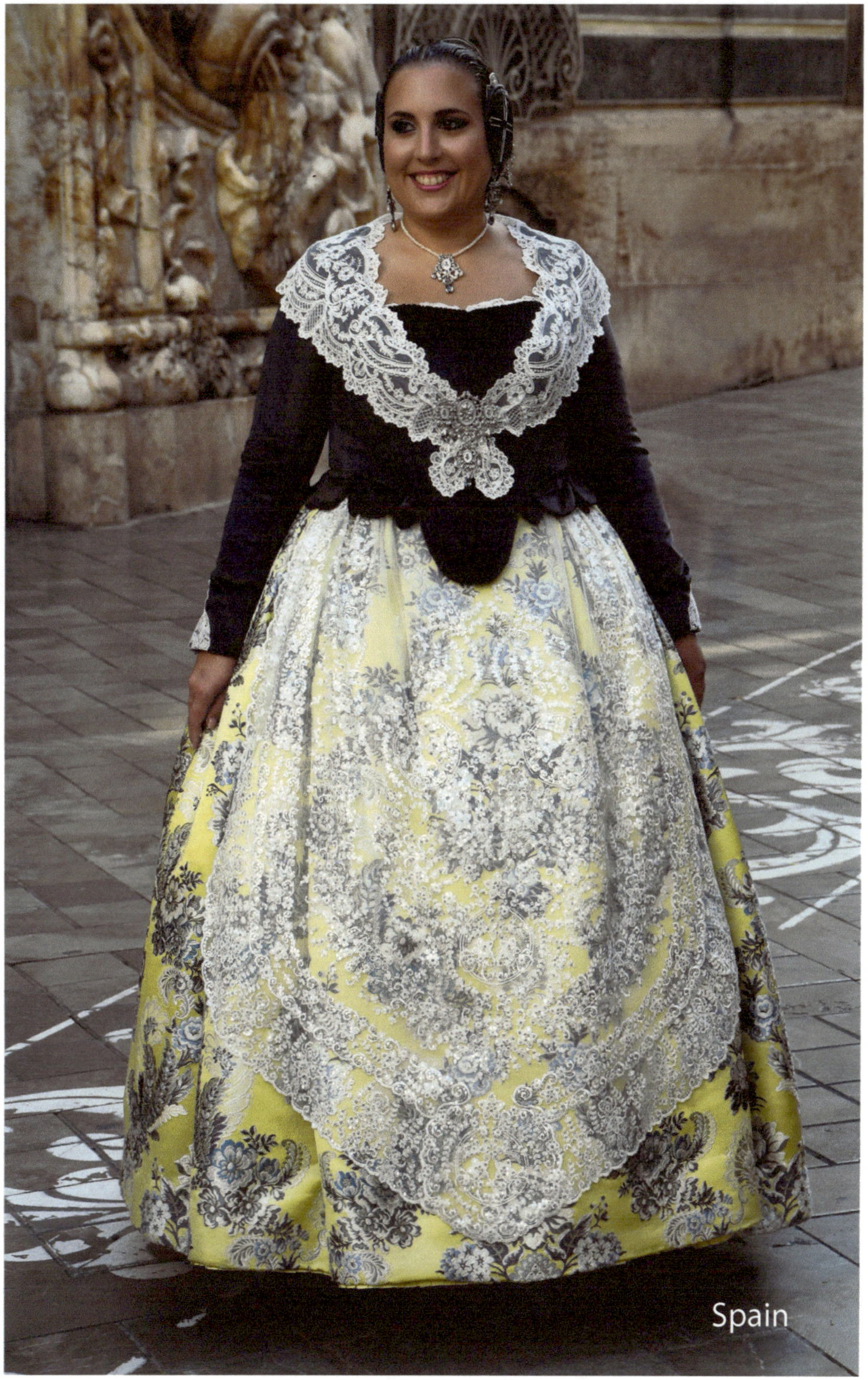

Spain

The abundance of wild and domestic creatures that share our world certainly creates photographic challenges. Their color, size, and activity require some physical agility to focus and compose before the subject moves on, often needing the use of a telephoto lens – once again readily available on cellphones.

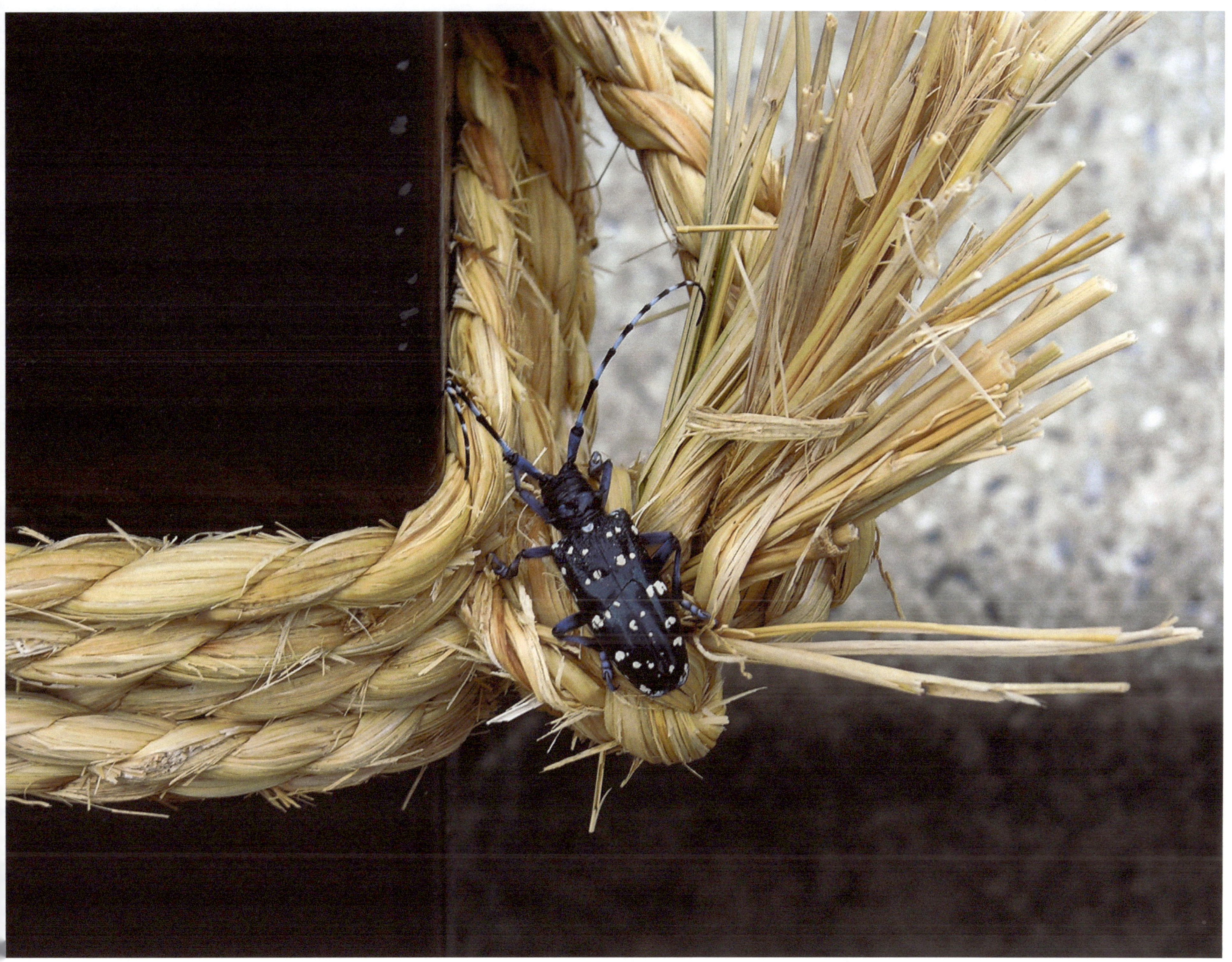

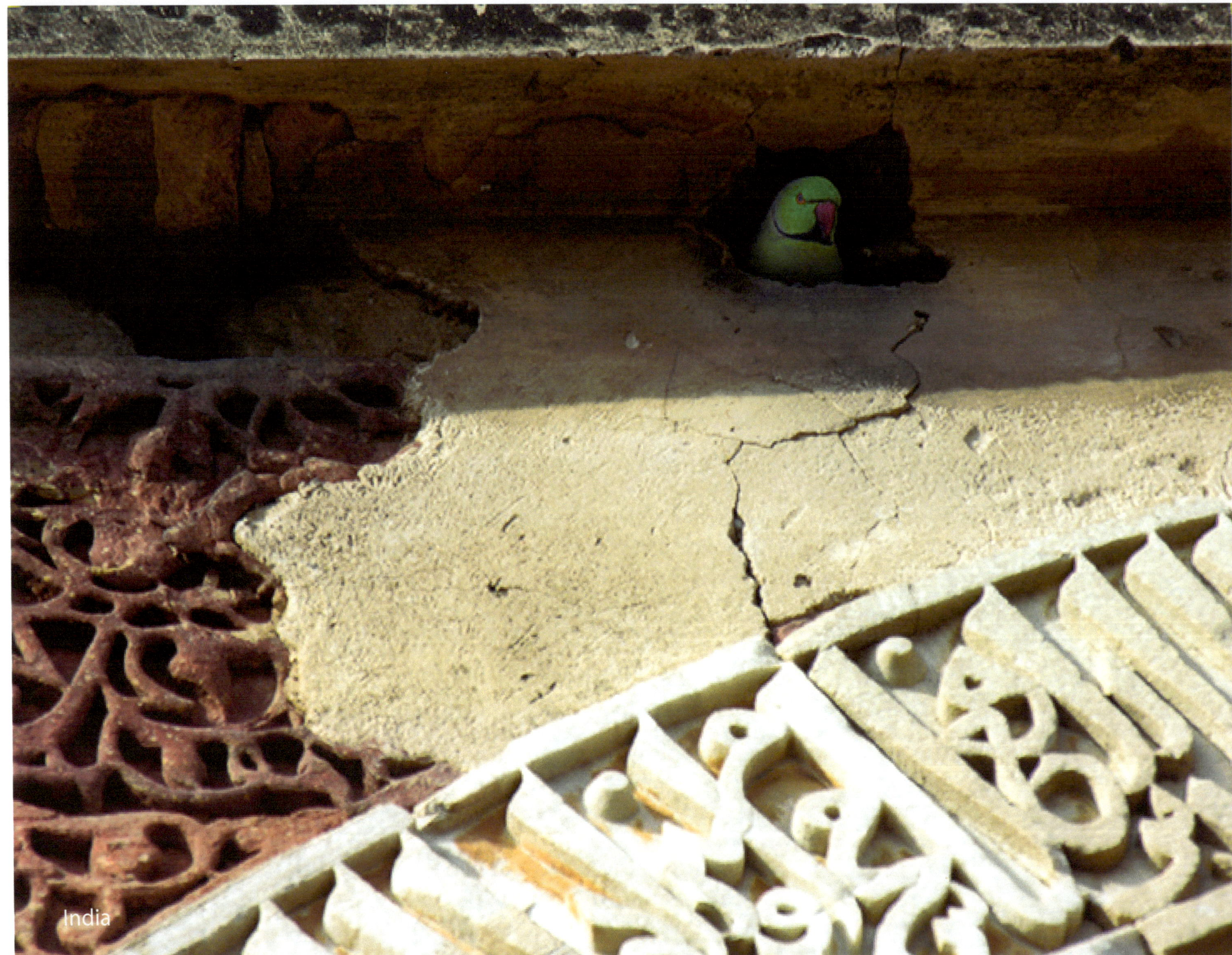
India

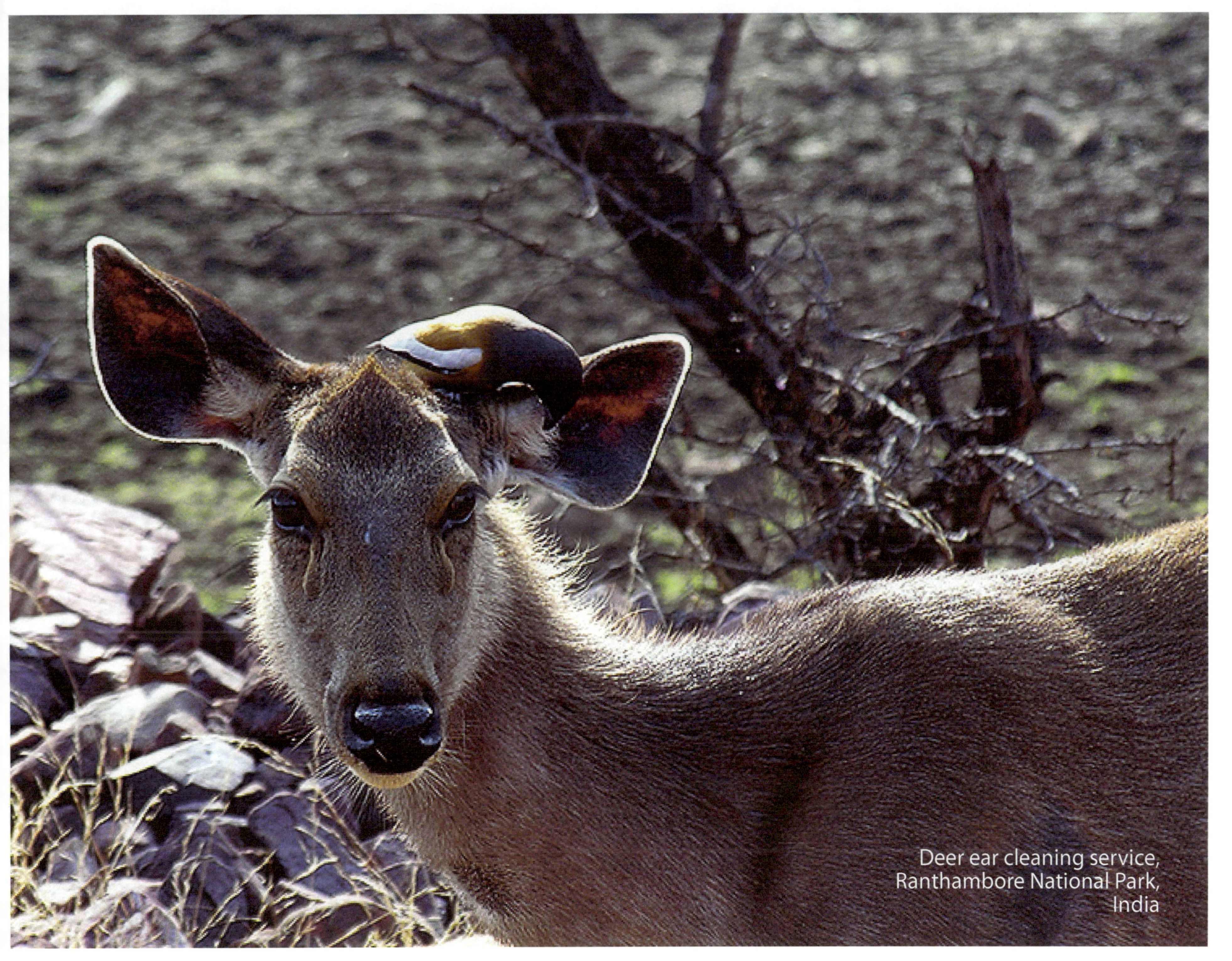

Deer ear cleaning service,
Ranthambore National Park,
India

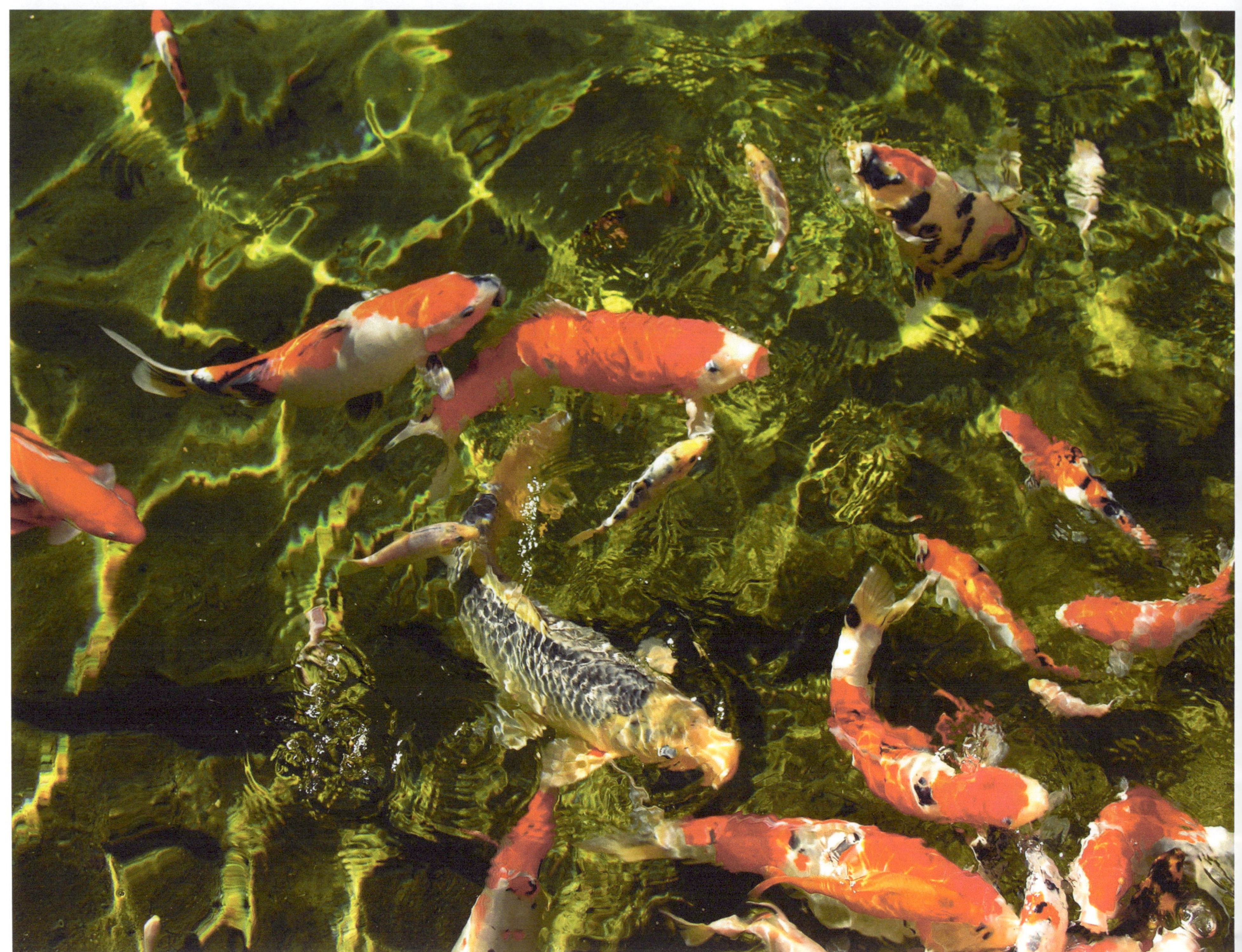

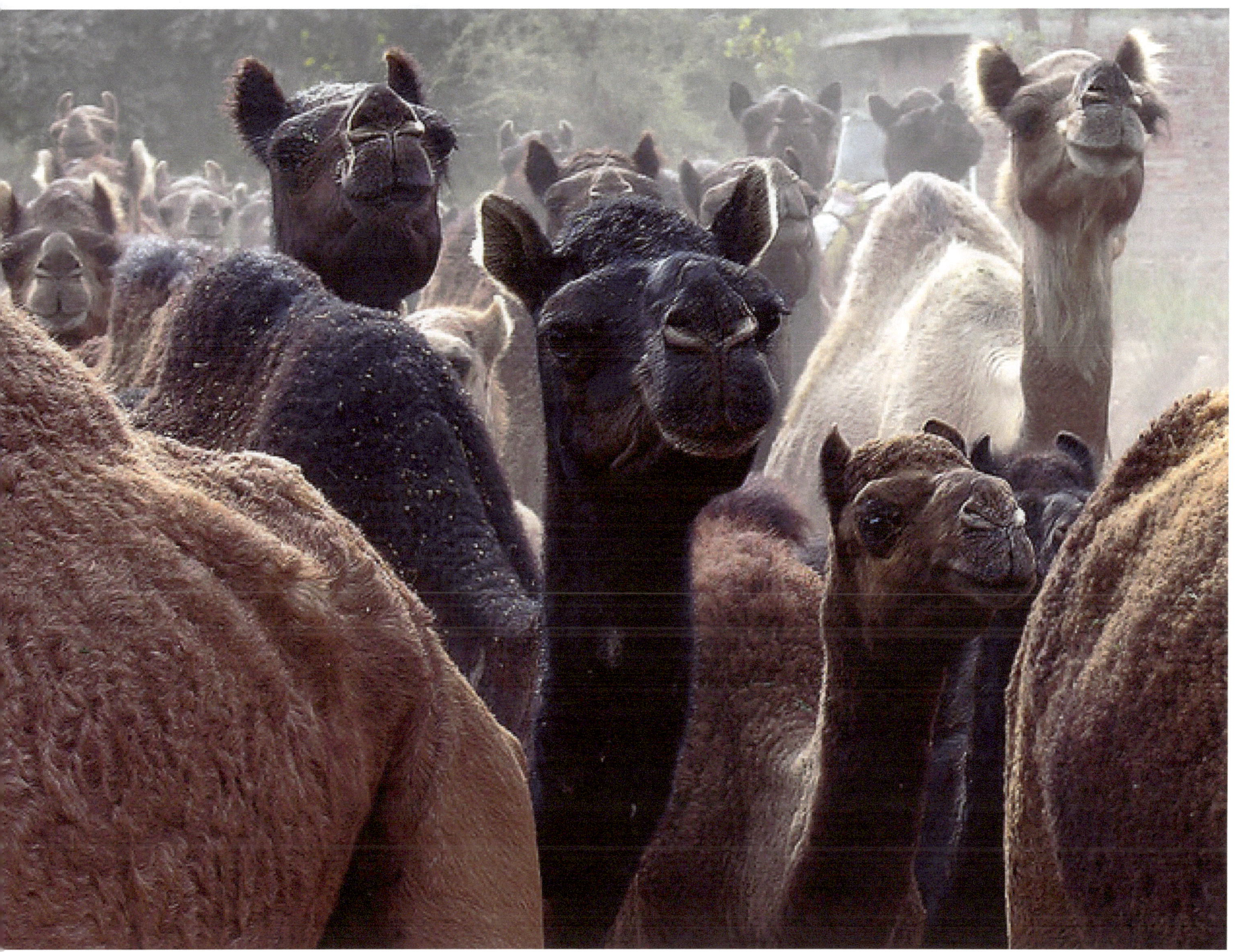

Our daily lives are surrounded by nature's flora as well as those we cultivate for sustenance, the health and well-being of our bodies. The beauty, color, and fragrance of the vast ecological biodiversity of wilderness areas provide solace and recreation. Their character is a natural attraction for photography.

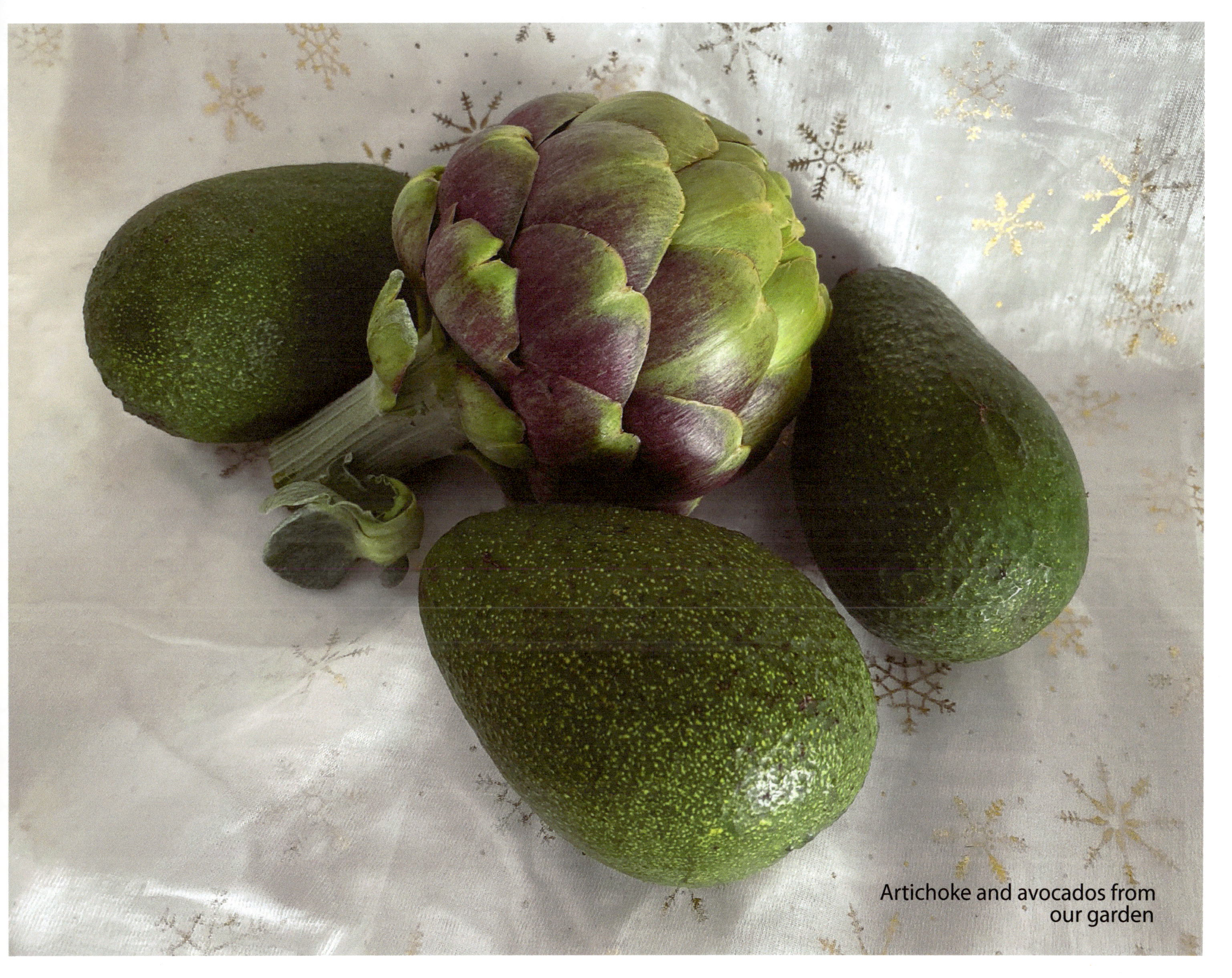

Artichoke and avocados from our garden

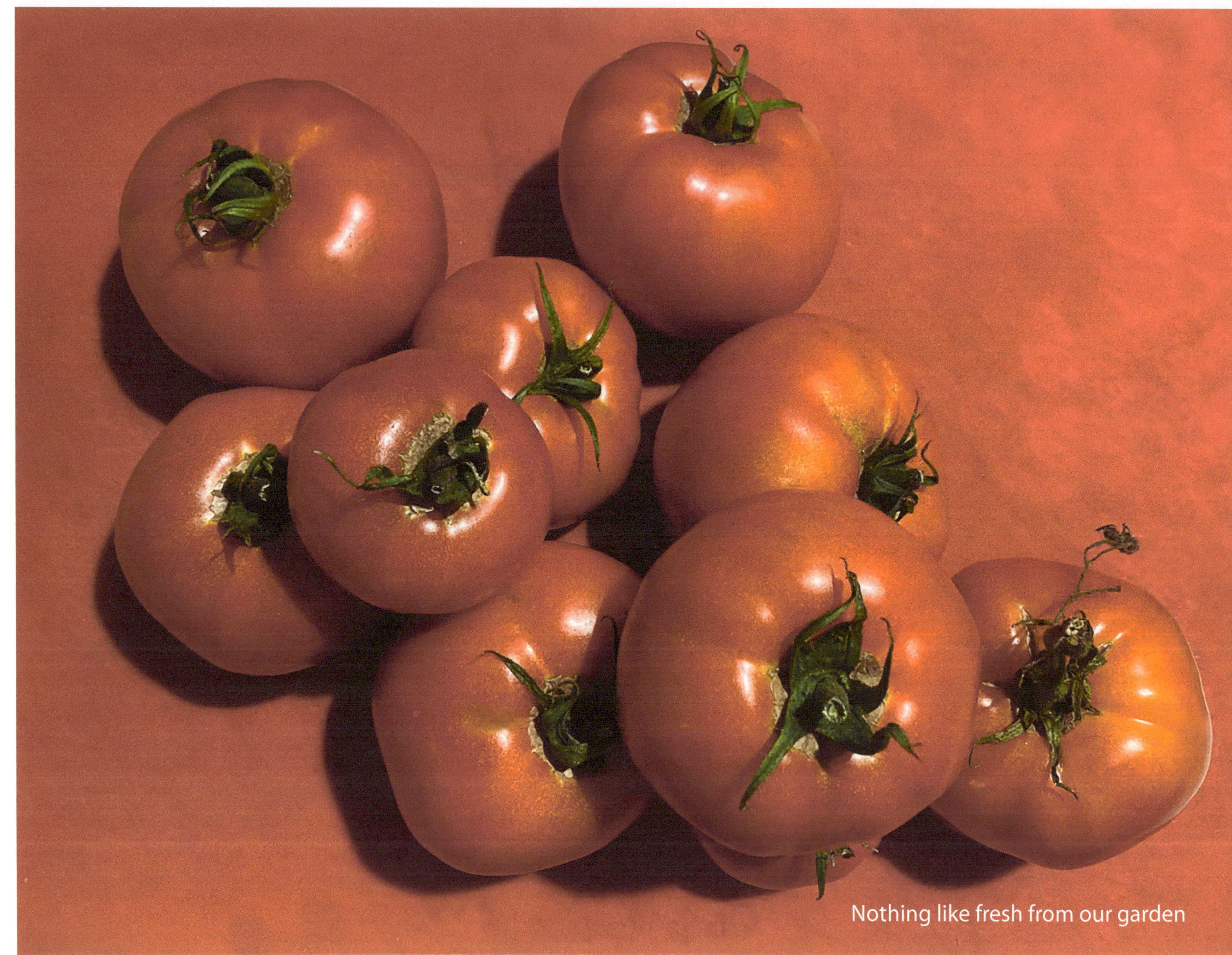
Nothing like fresh from our garden

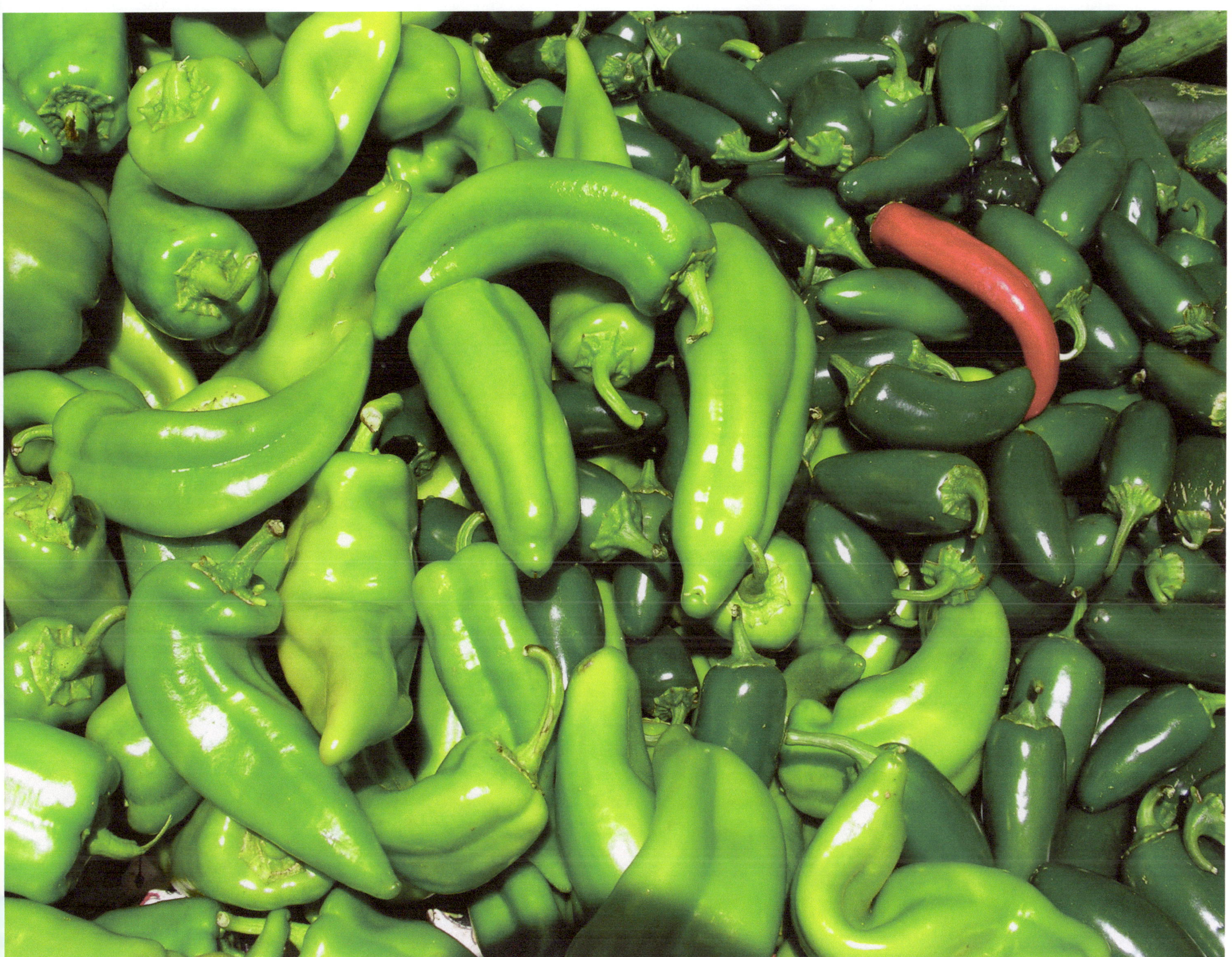

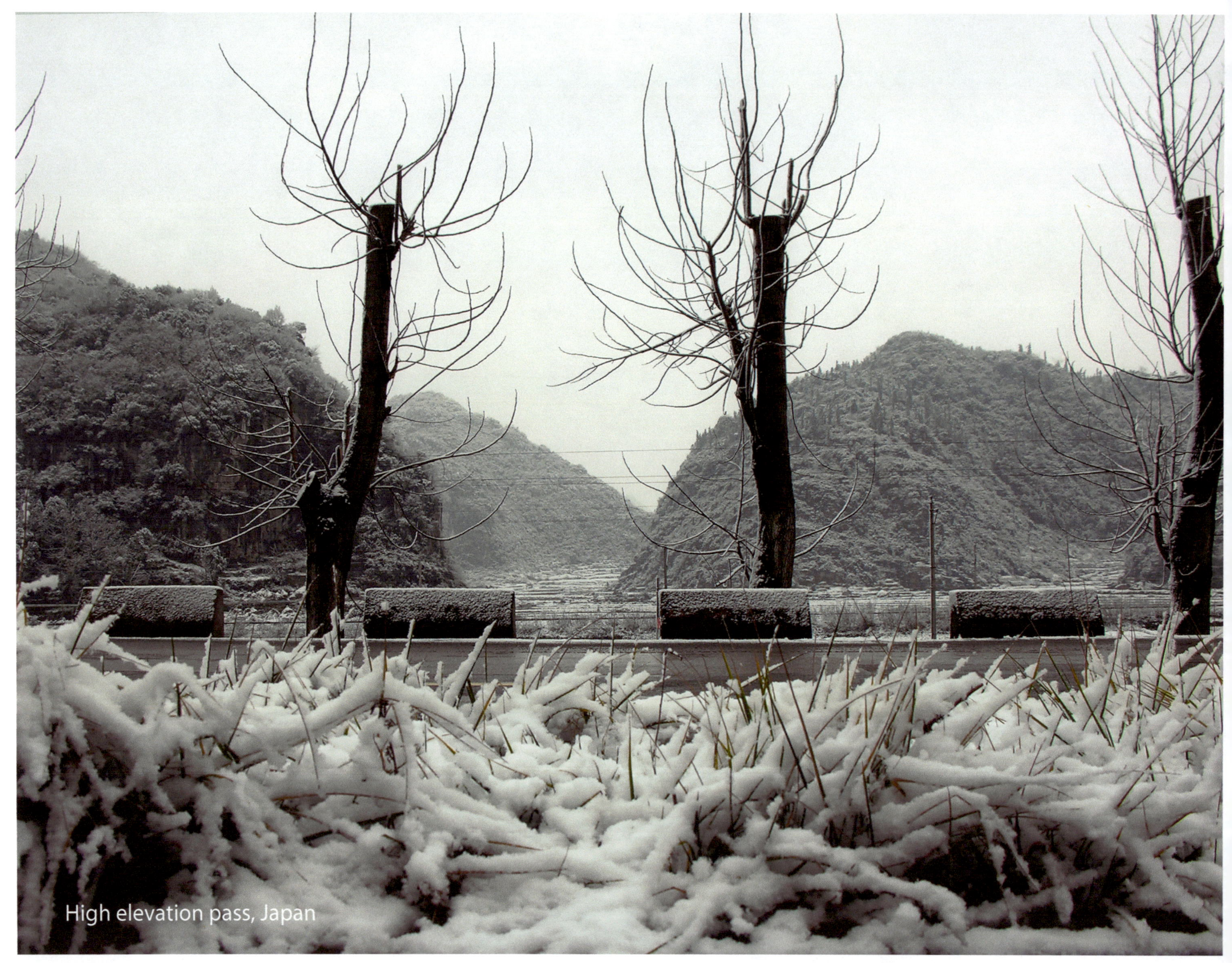
High elevation pass, Japan

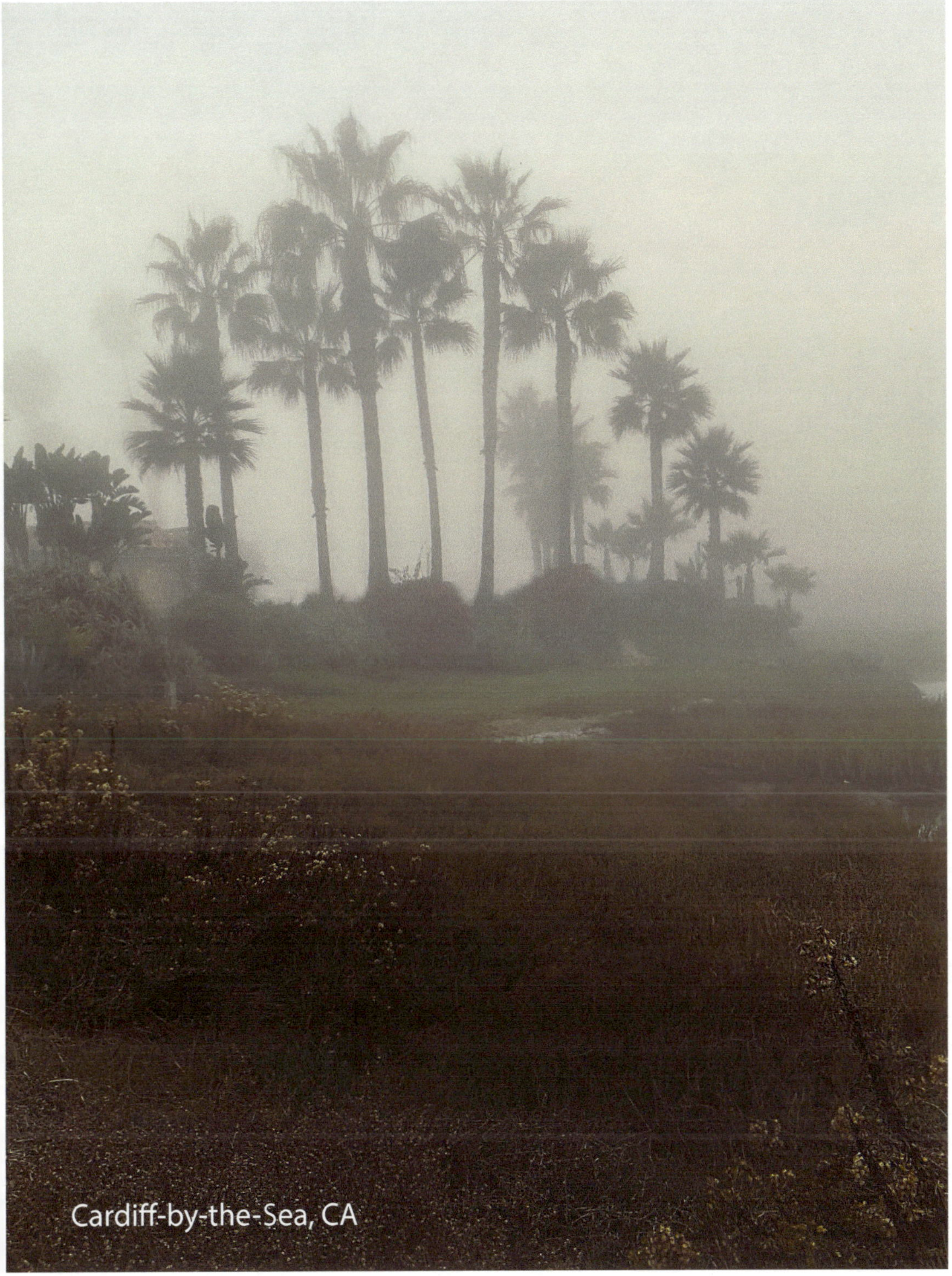

Cardiff-by-the-Sea, CA

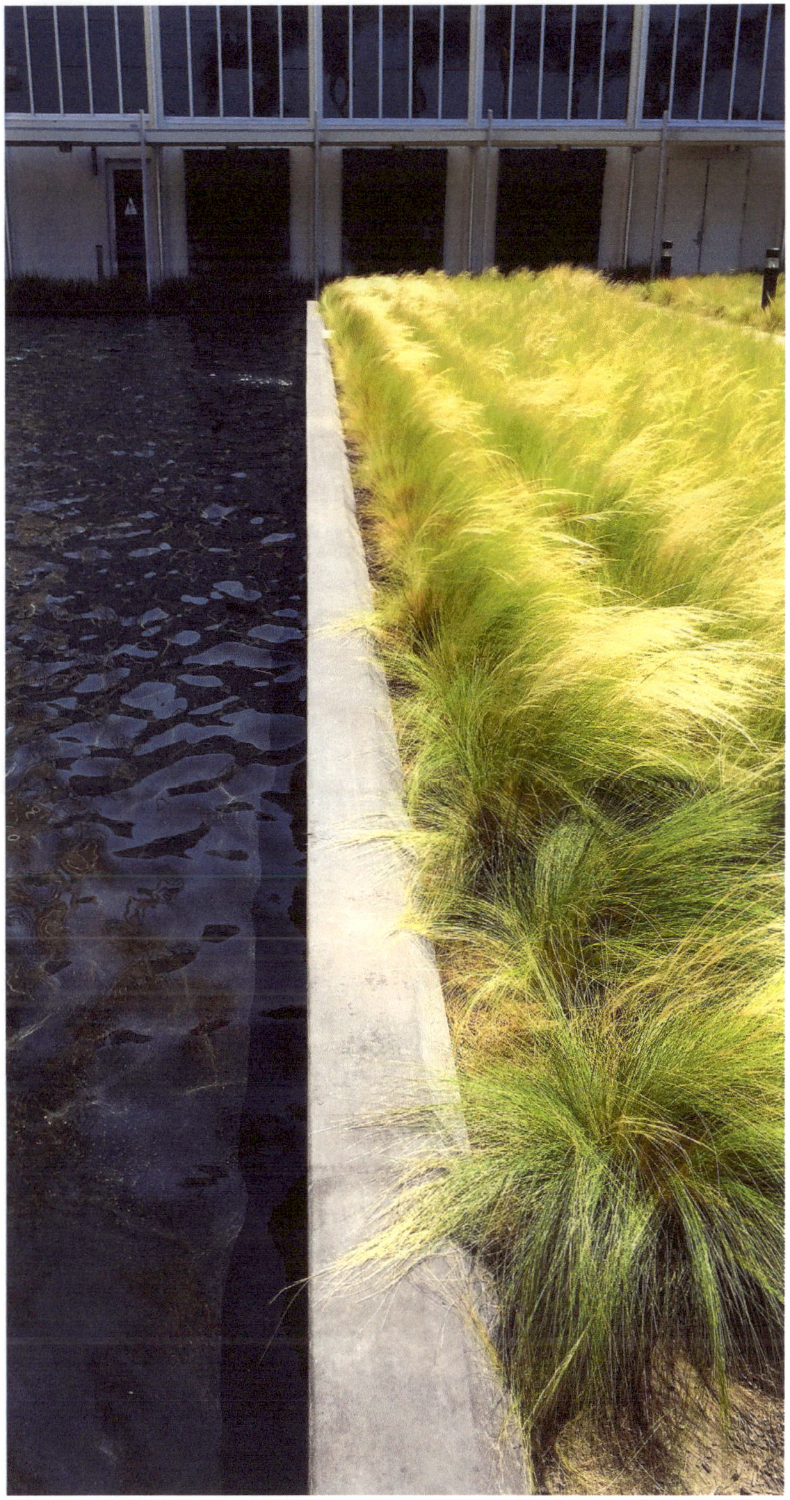

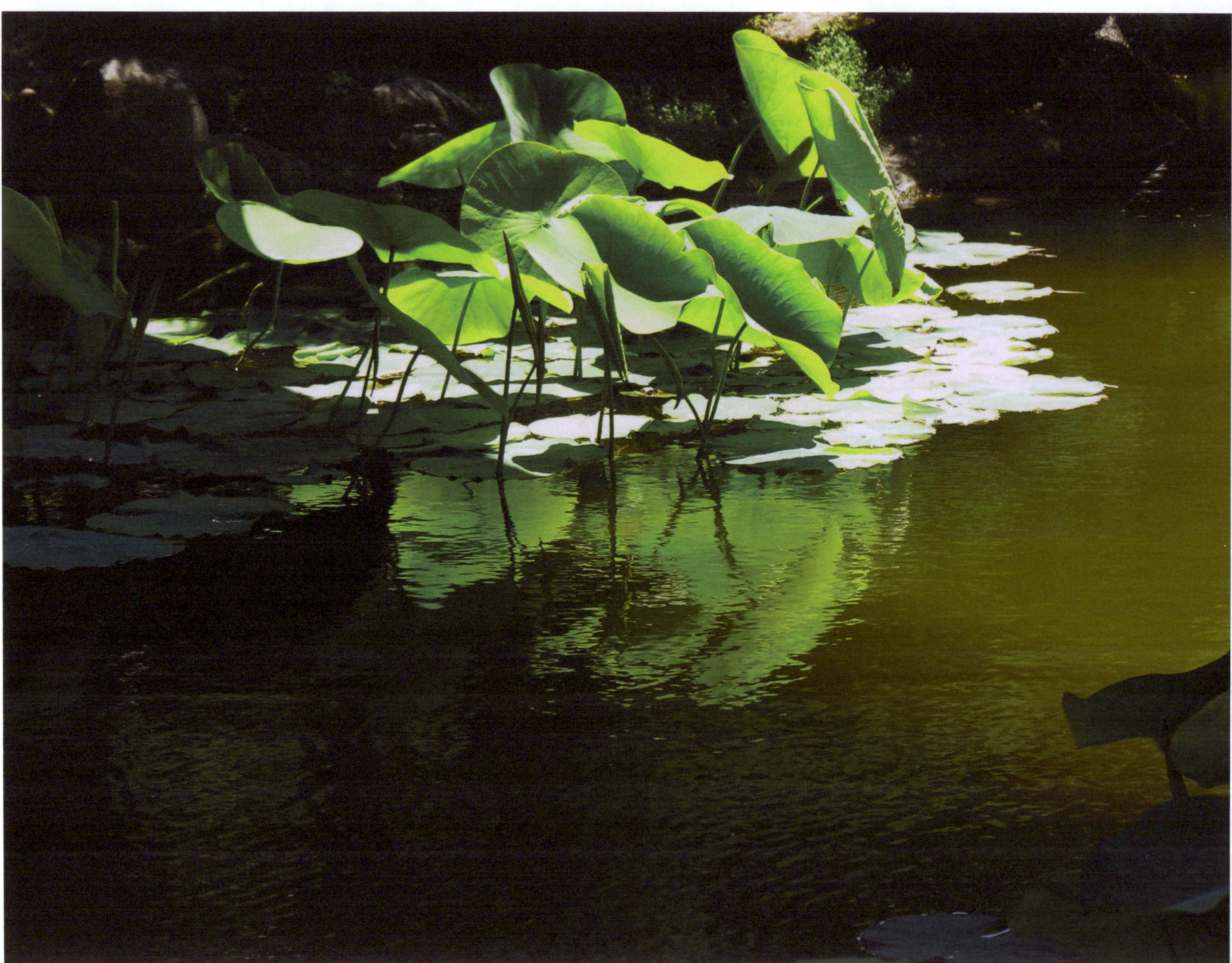

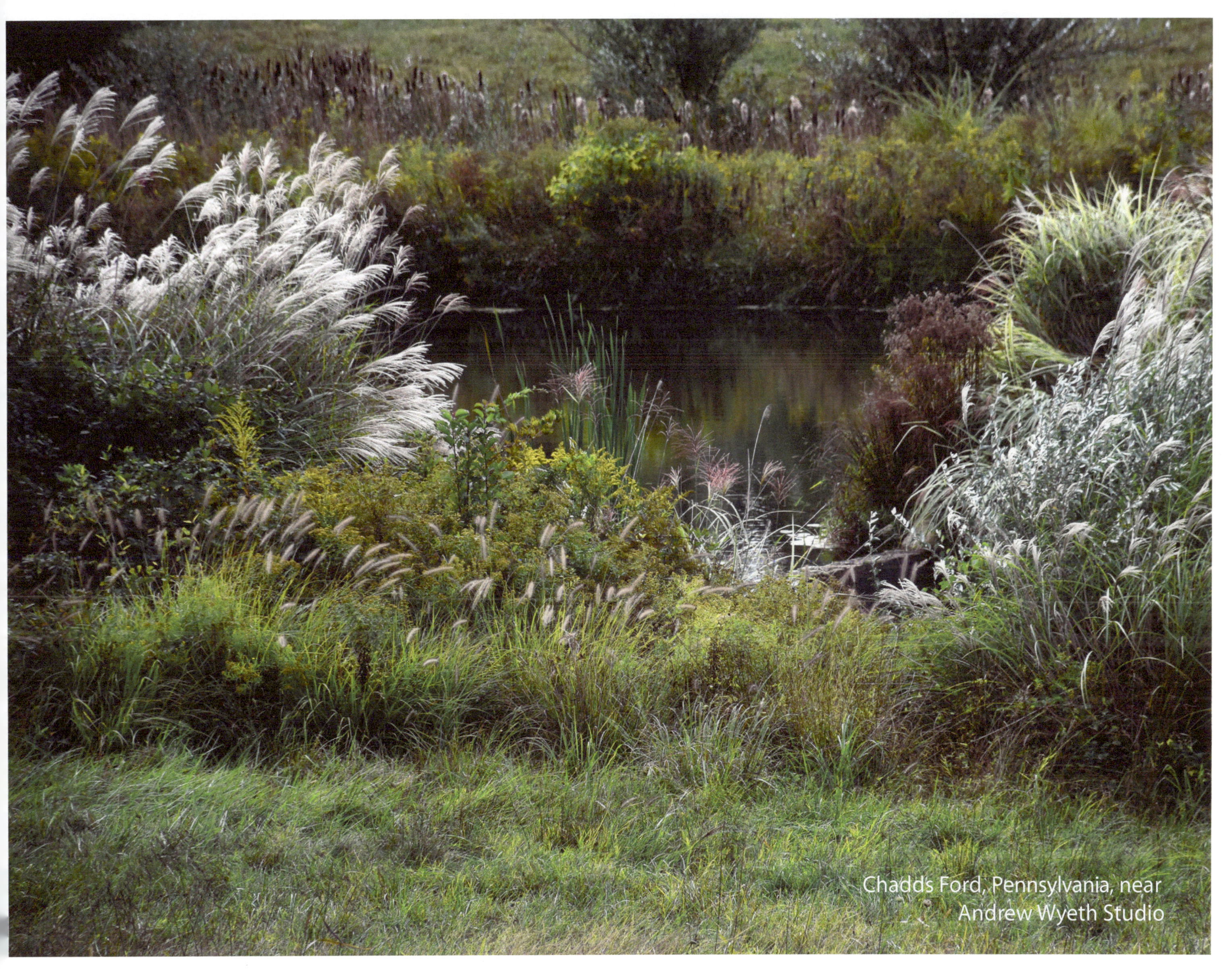

Chadd's Ford, Pennsylvania, near
Andrew Wyeth Studio

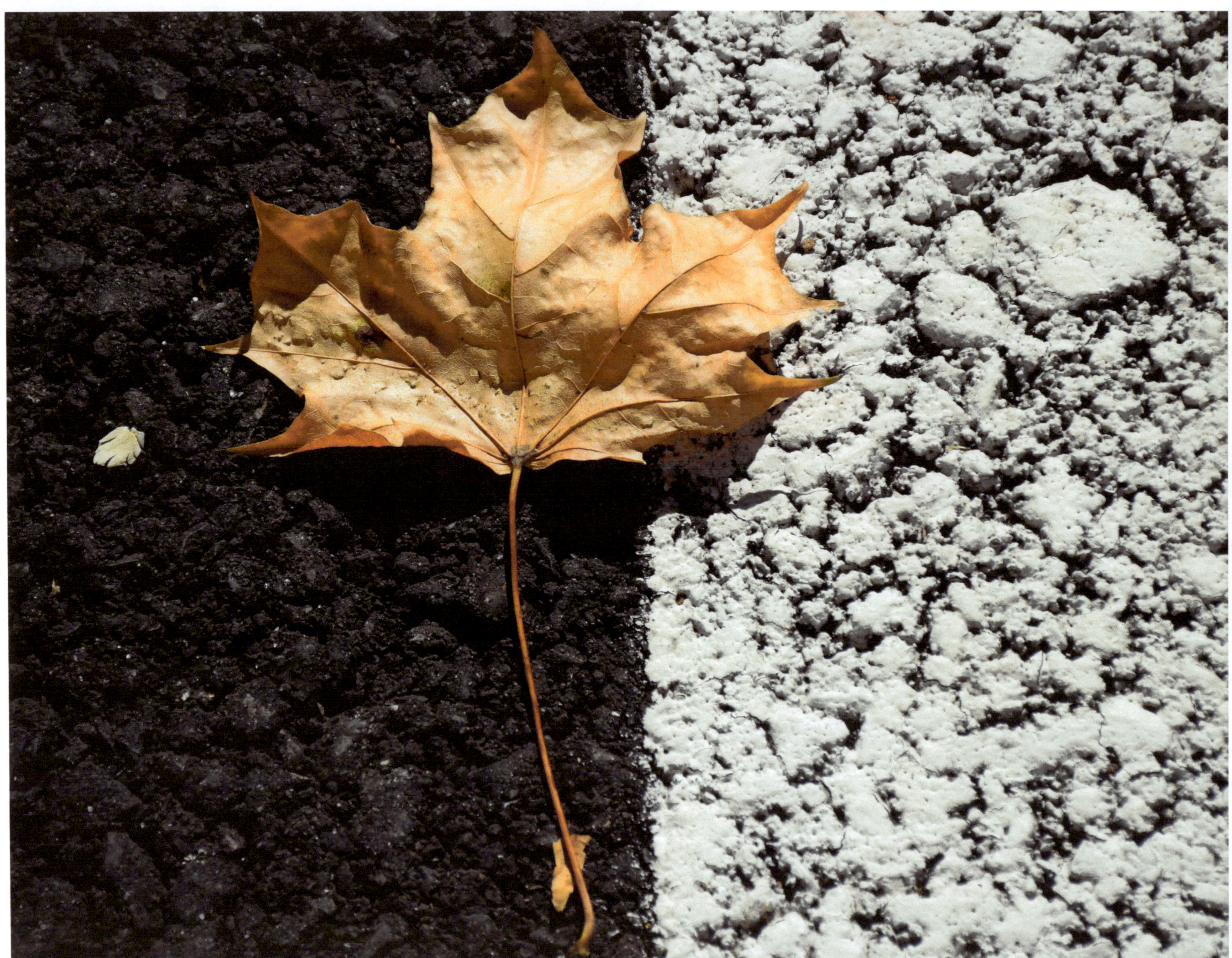

*Photography
takes an instant out of time,
altering life
by holding it still.*

– Dorothea Lange

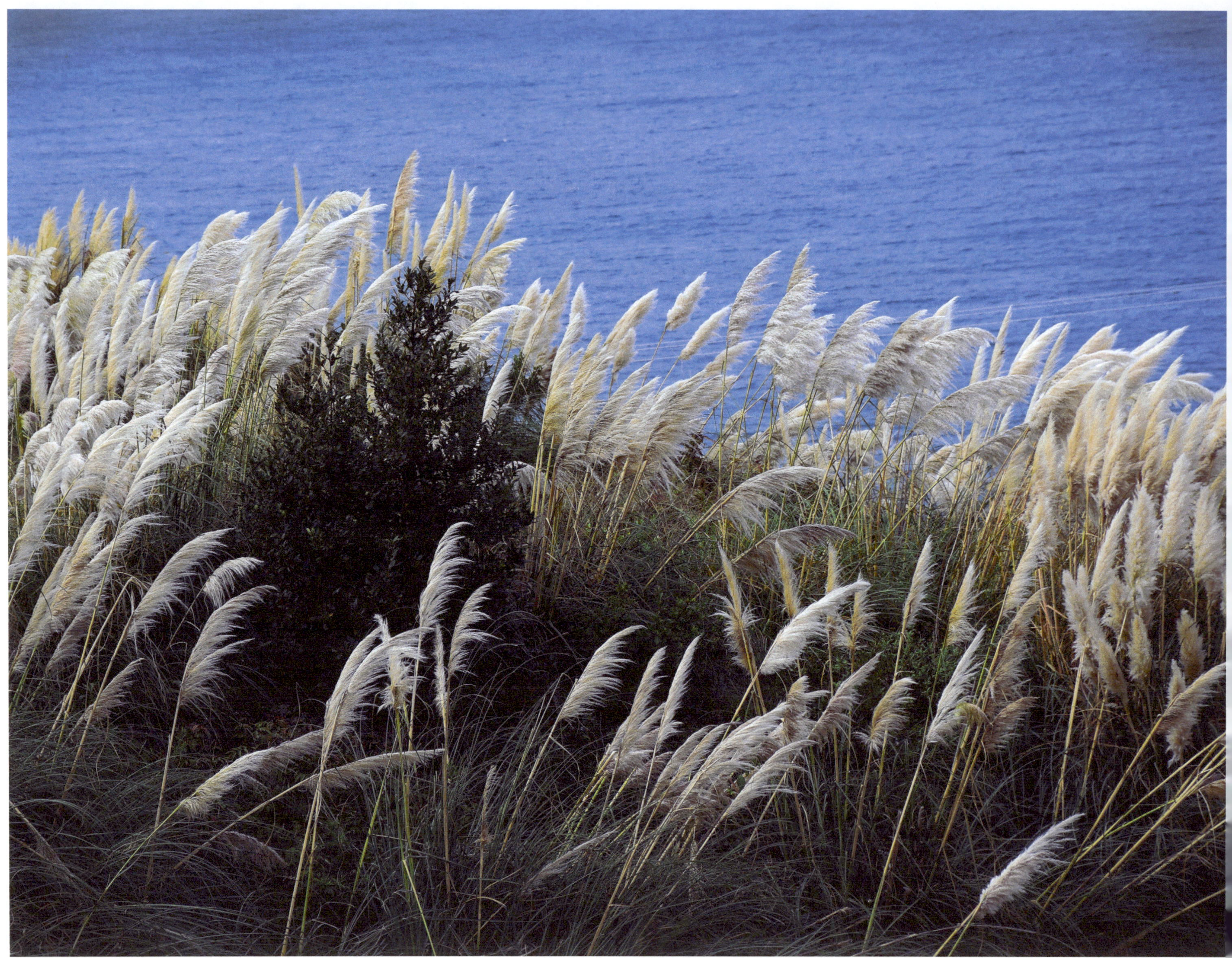

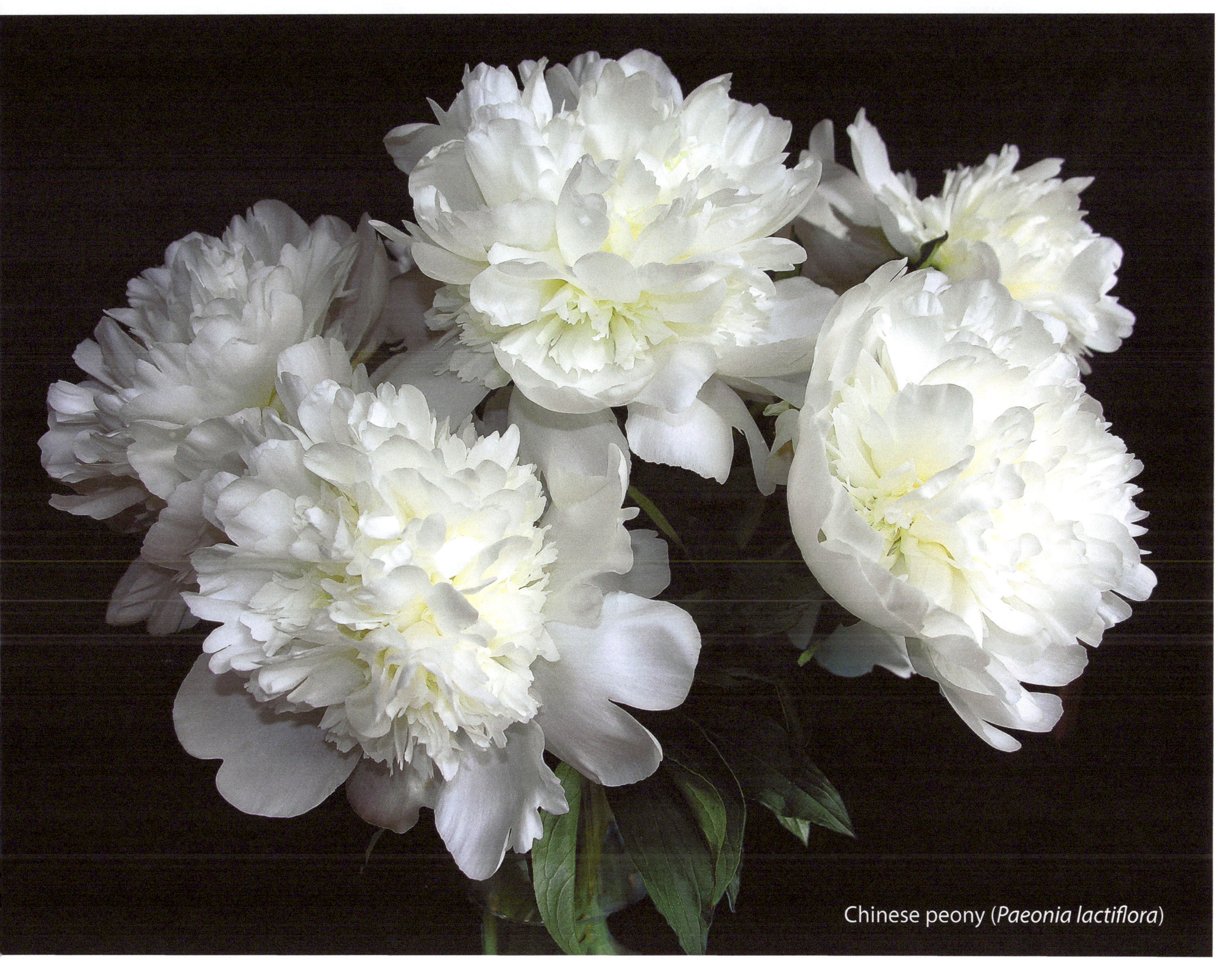

Chinese peony (*Paeonia lactiflora*)

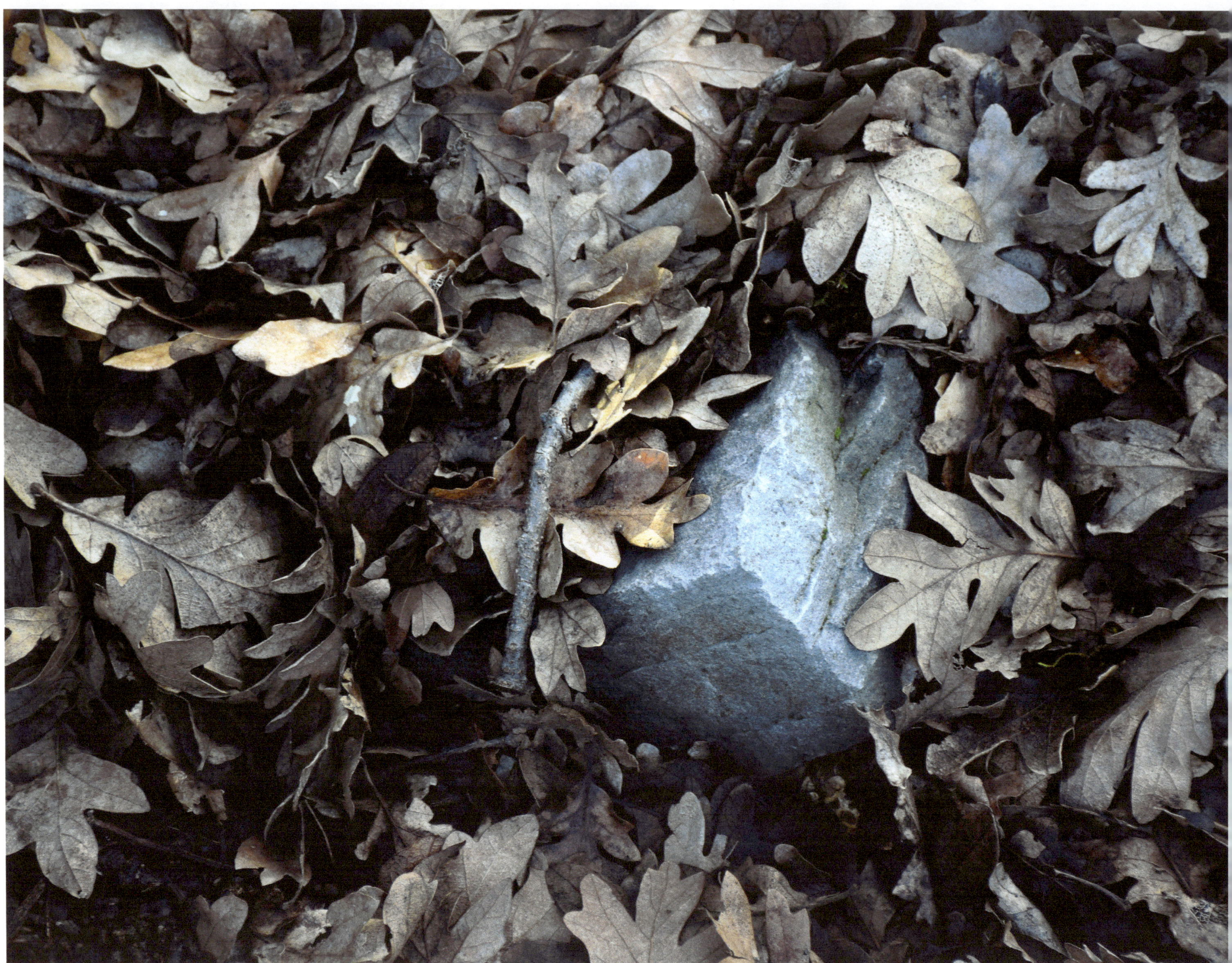

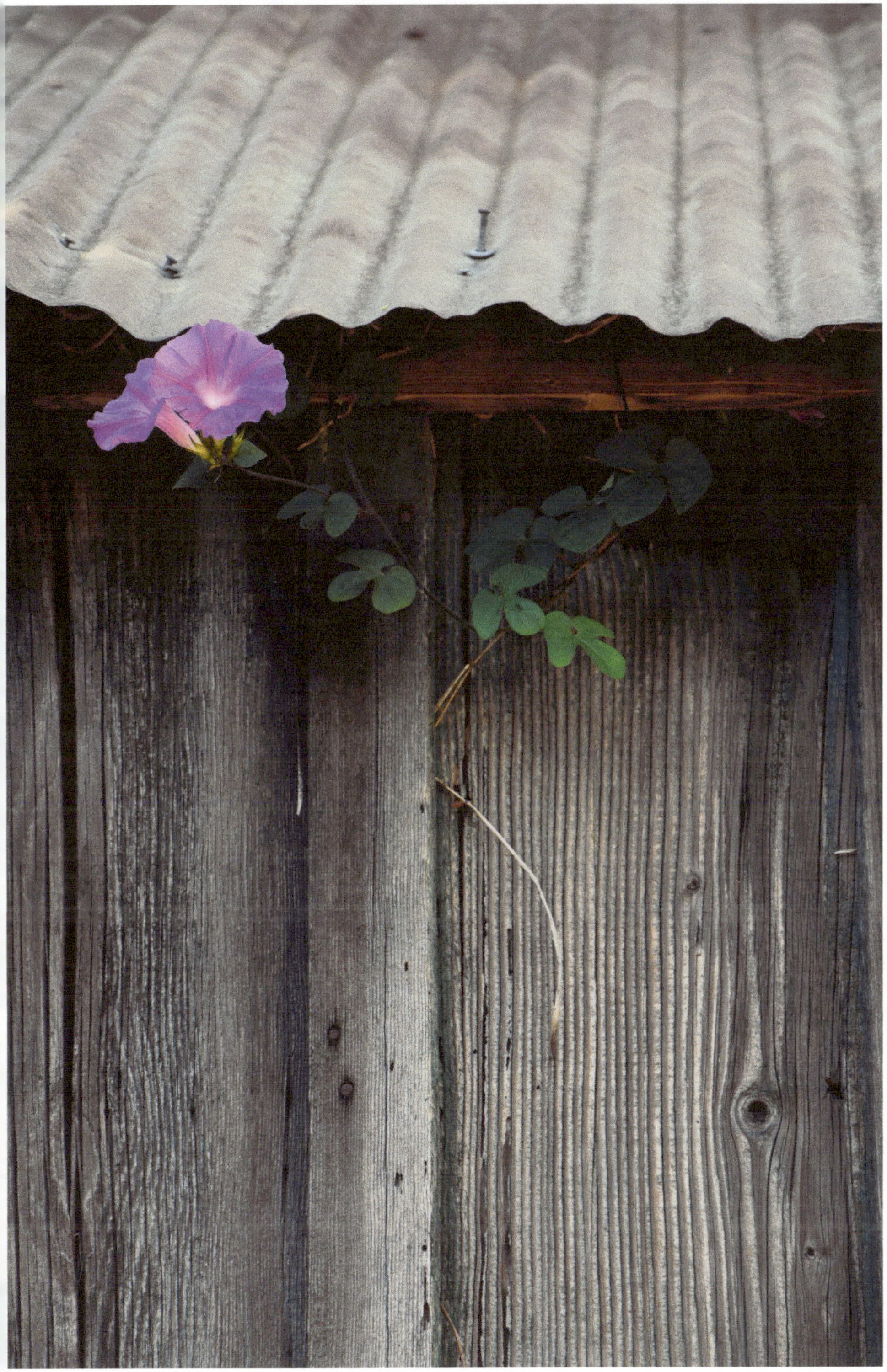

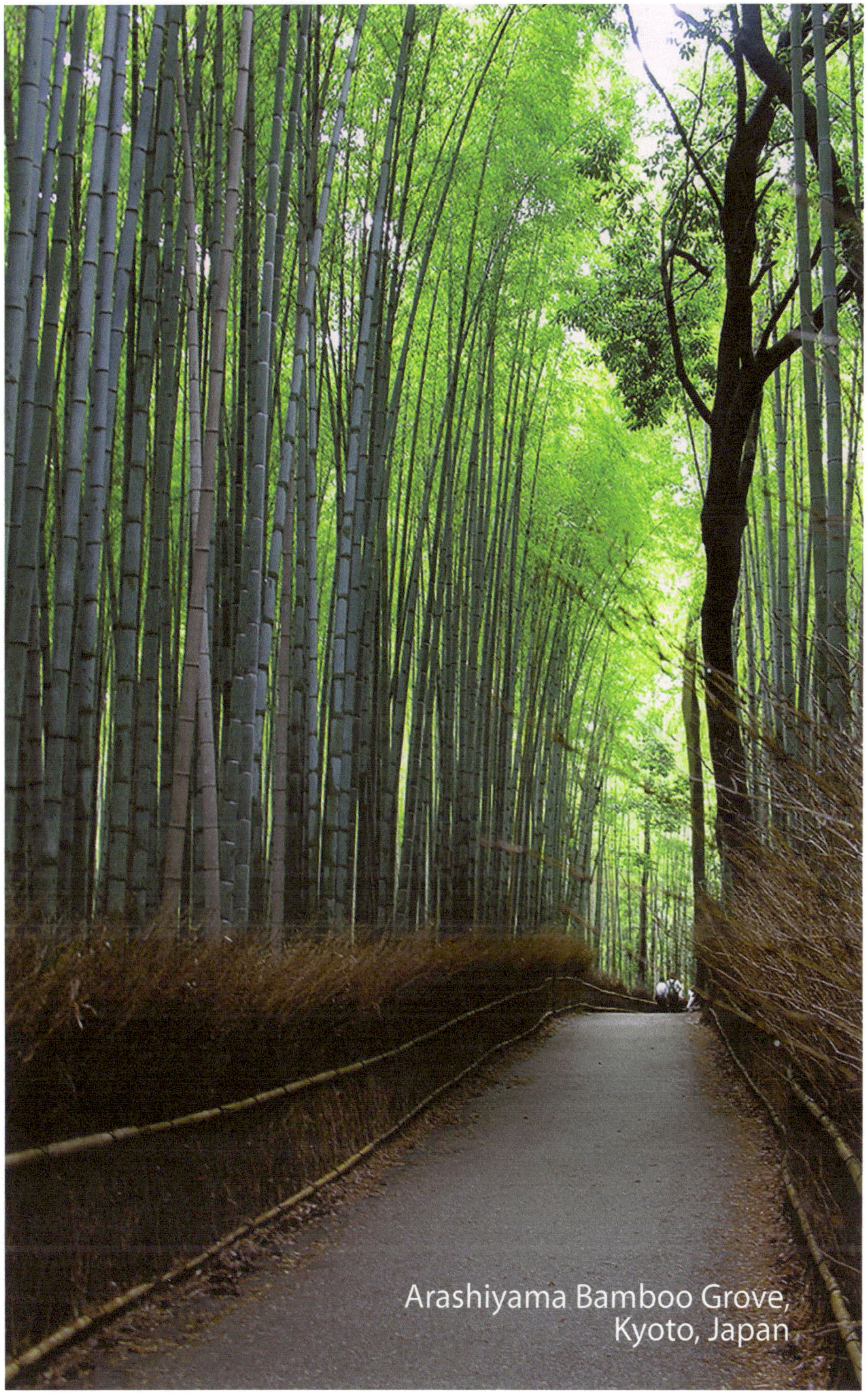

Arashiyama Bamboo Grove,
Kyoto, Japan

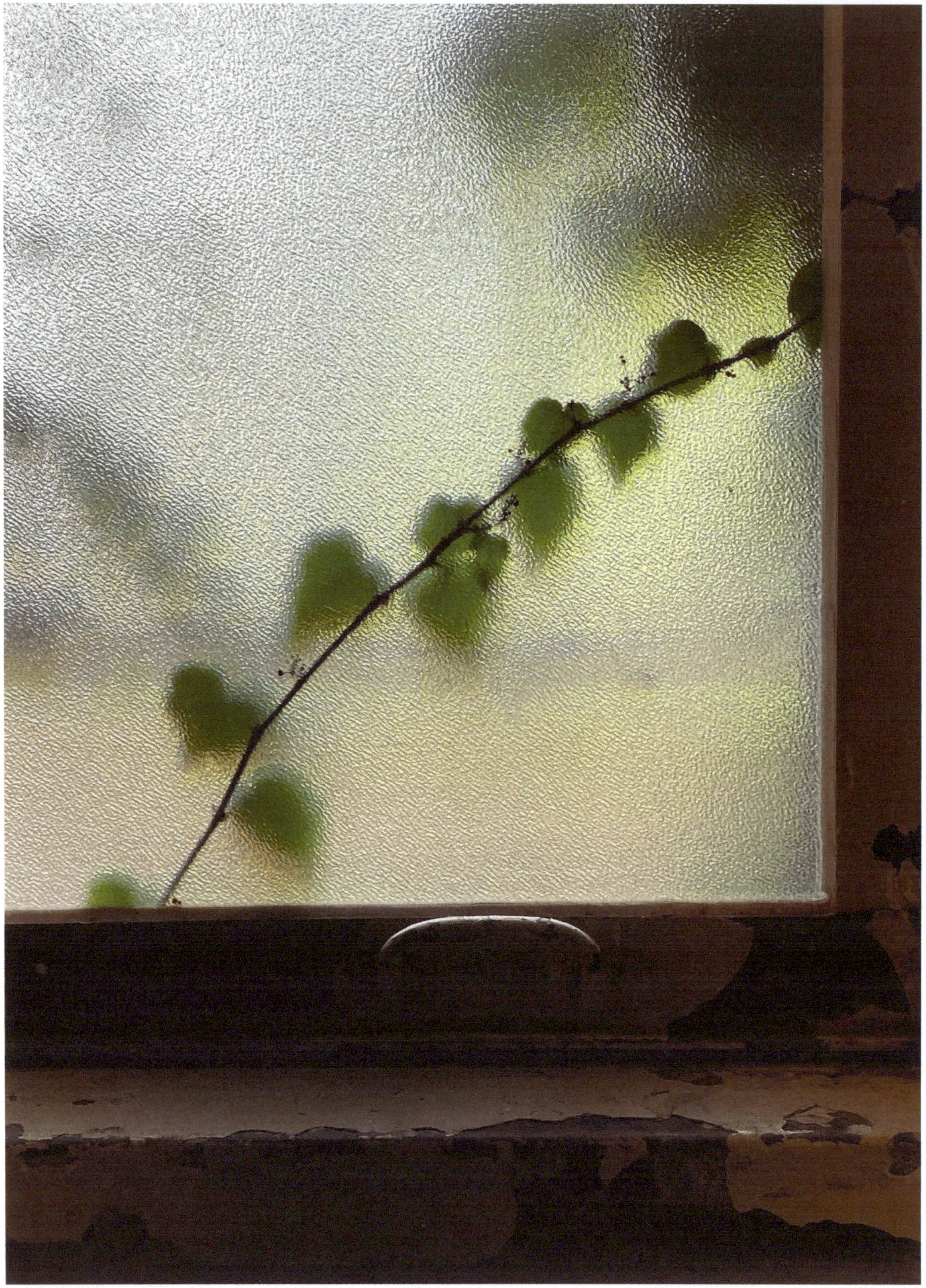

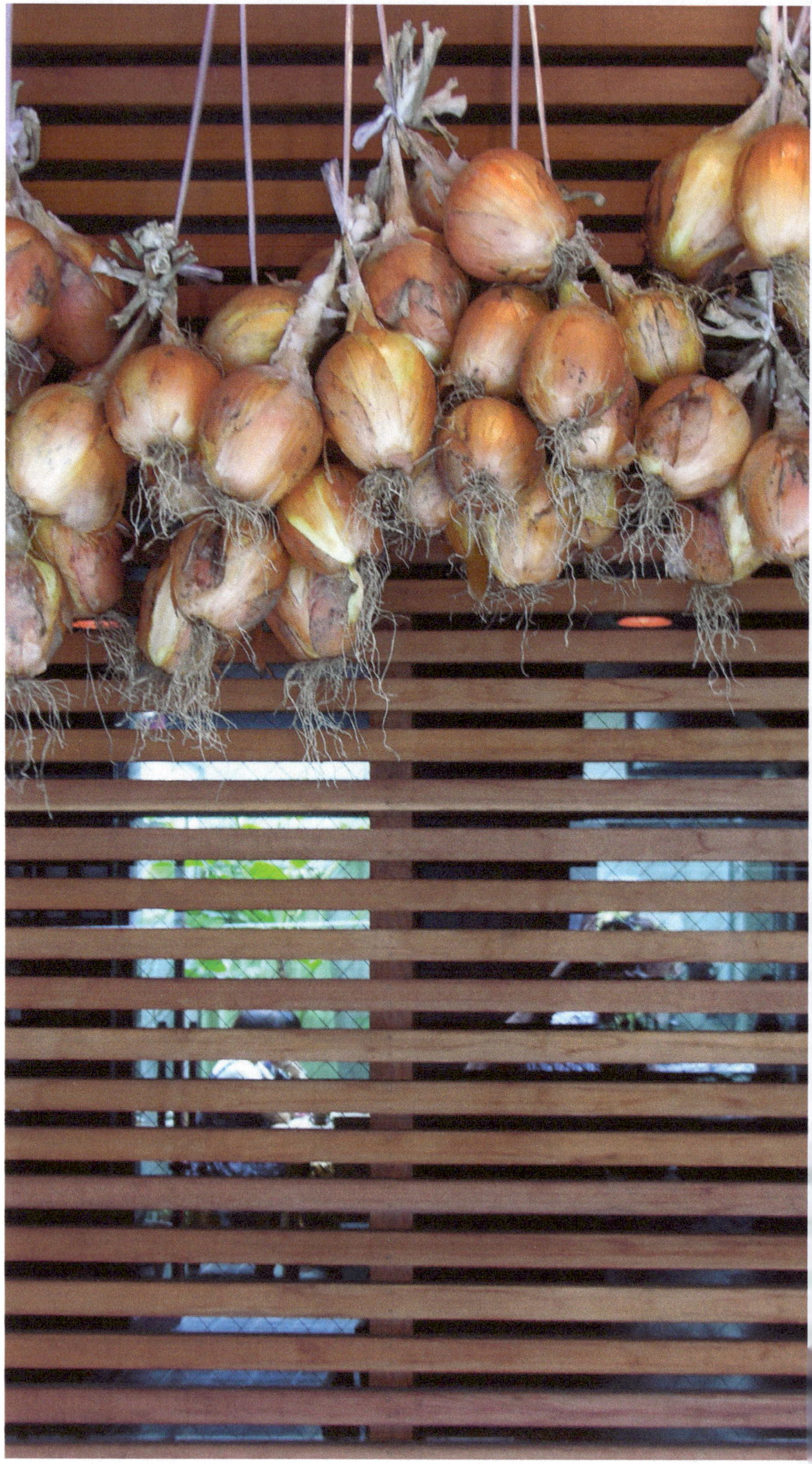

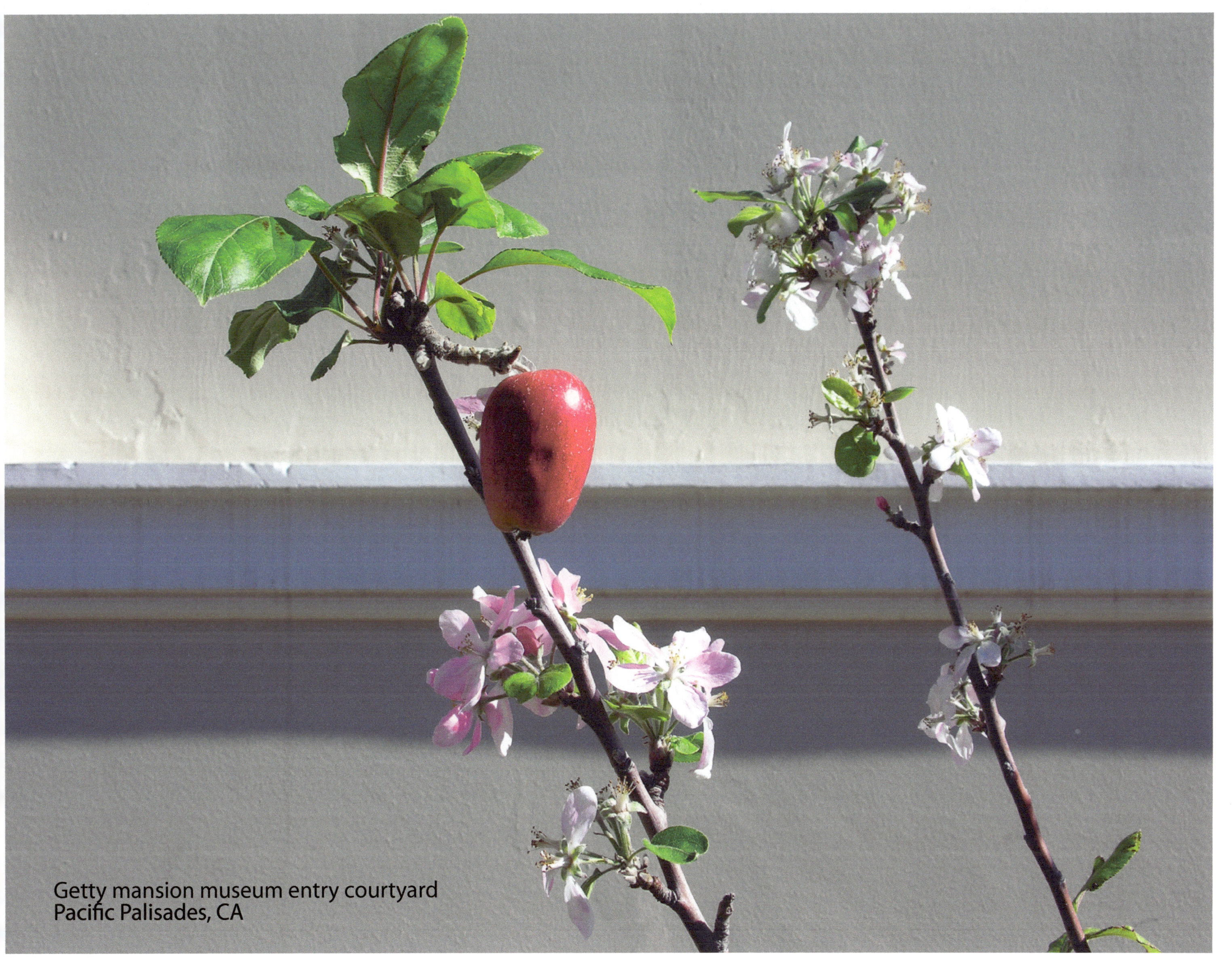

Getty mansion museum entry courtyard
Pacific Palisades, CA

To me, photography is an art
of observation.
It's about finding something interesting
in an ordinary place...
I've found it has little to do
with the things you see
and everything to do with
the way you see them.

-Elliott Erwitt

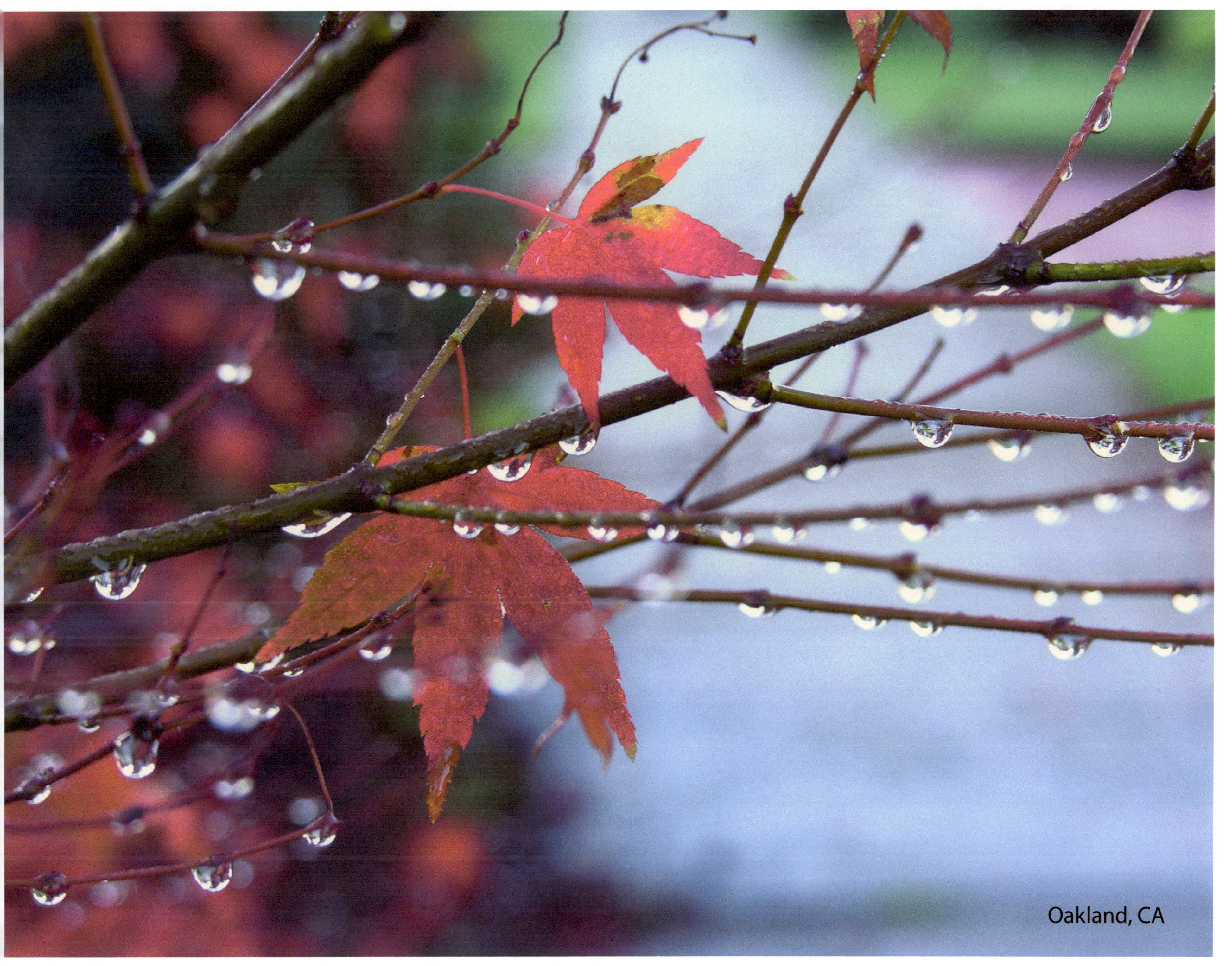
Oakland, CA

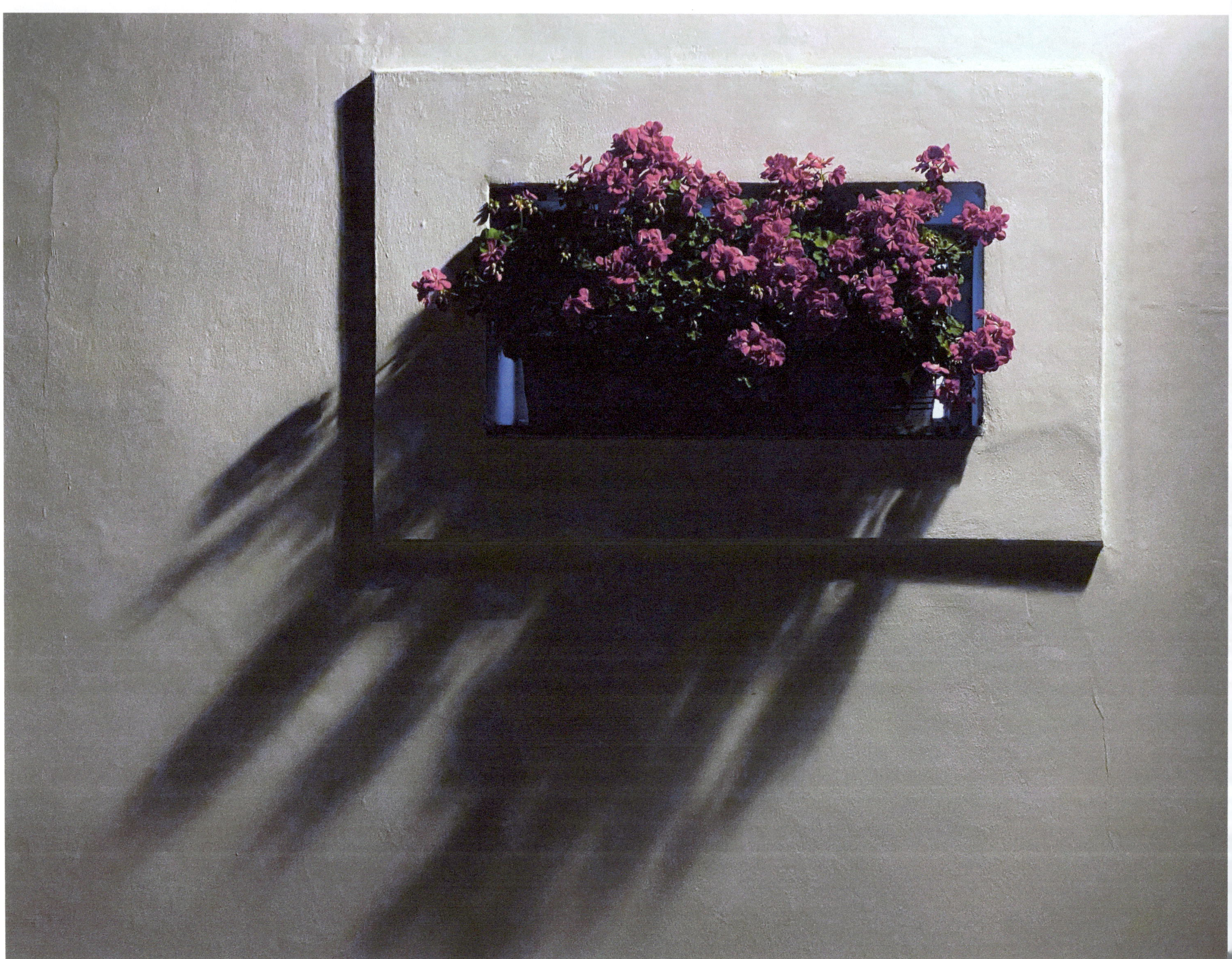

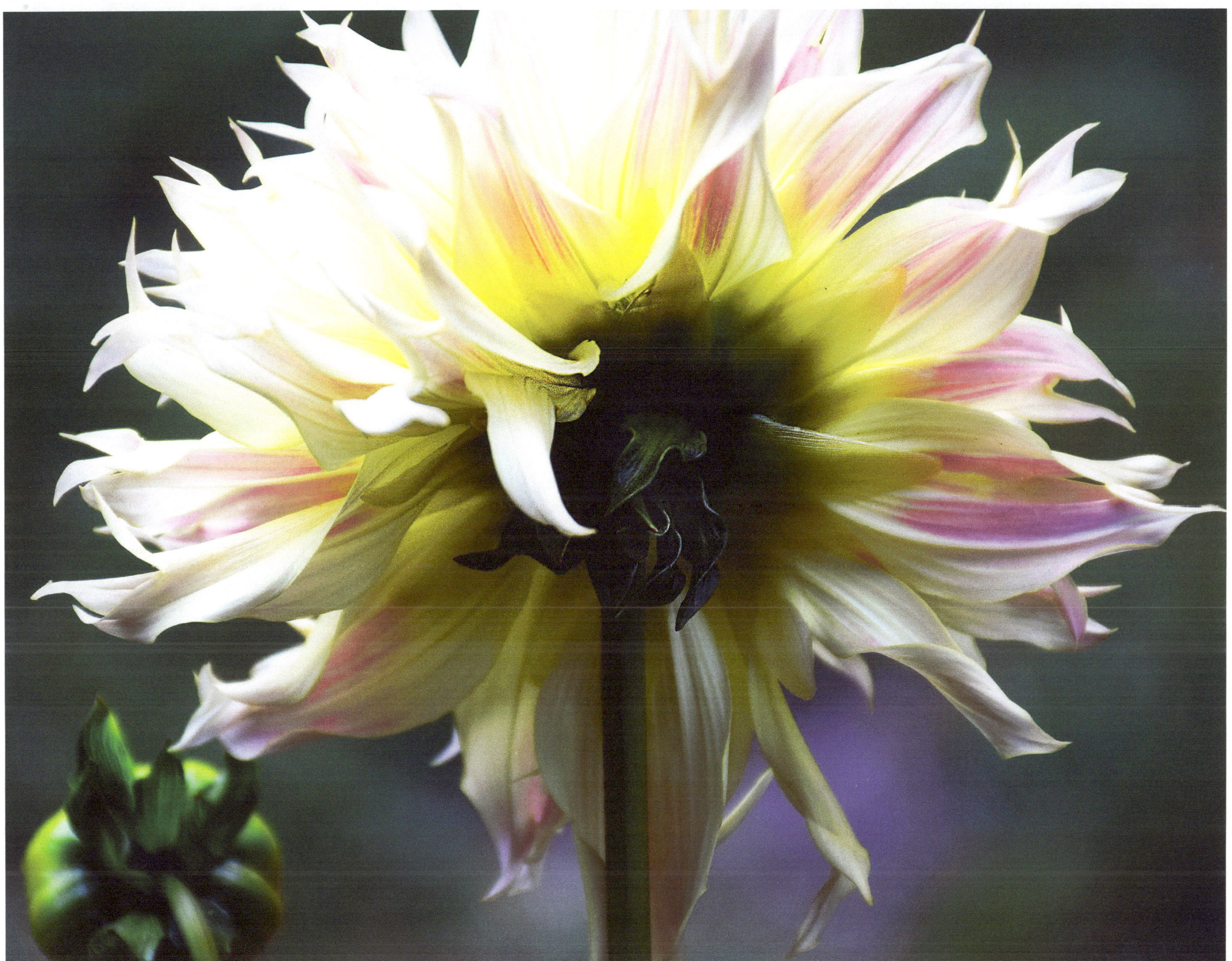

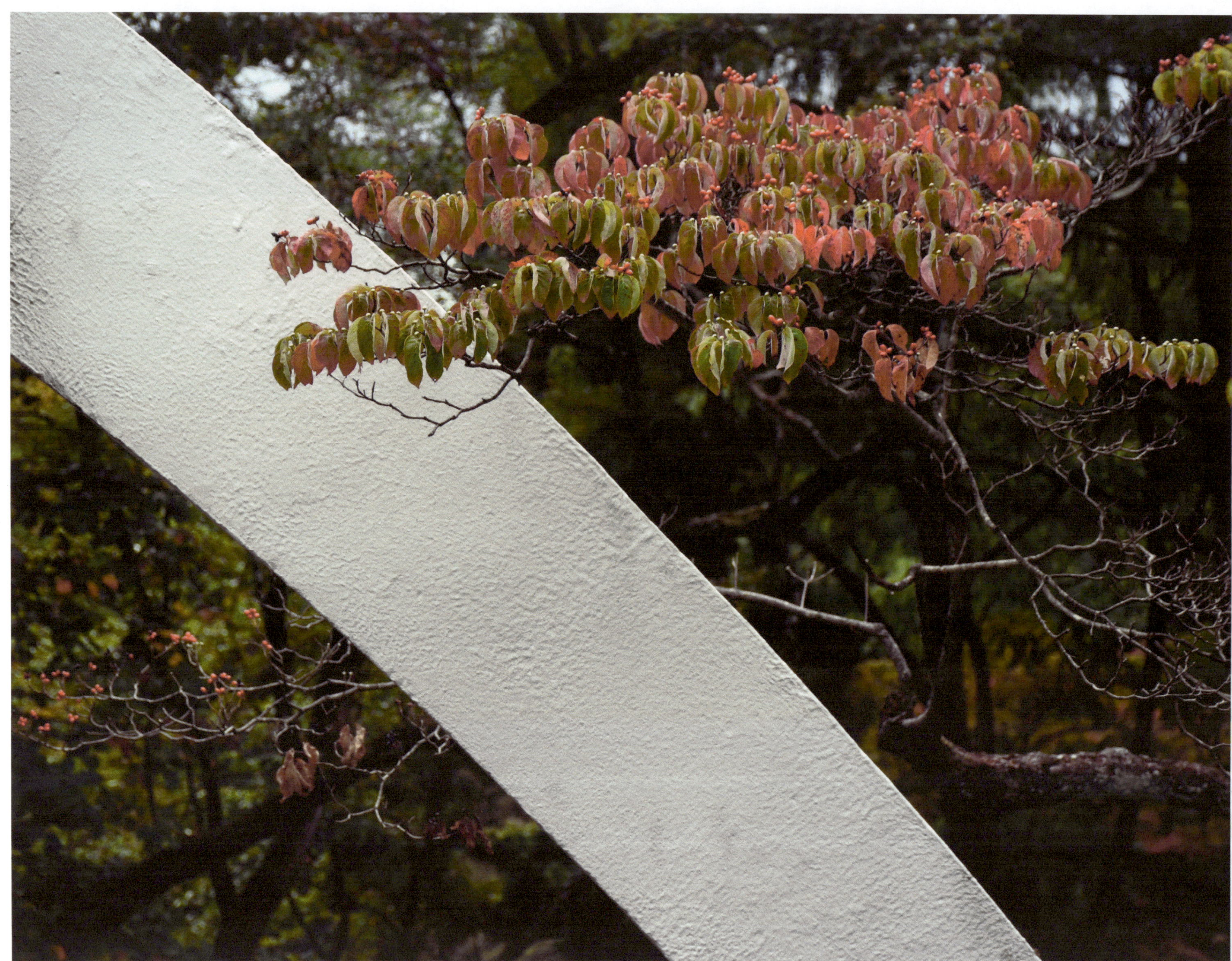

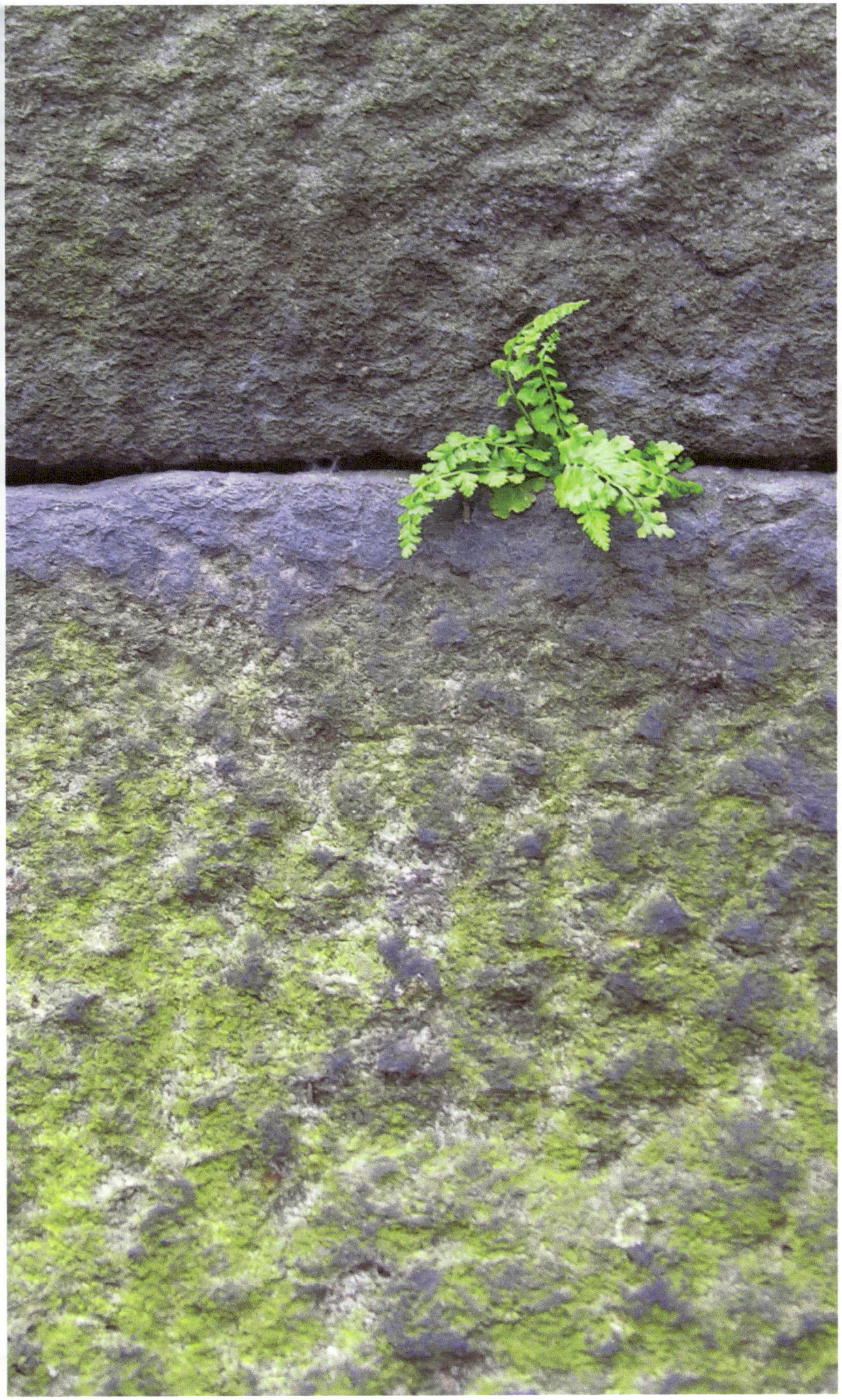

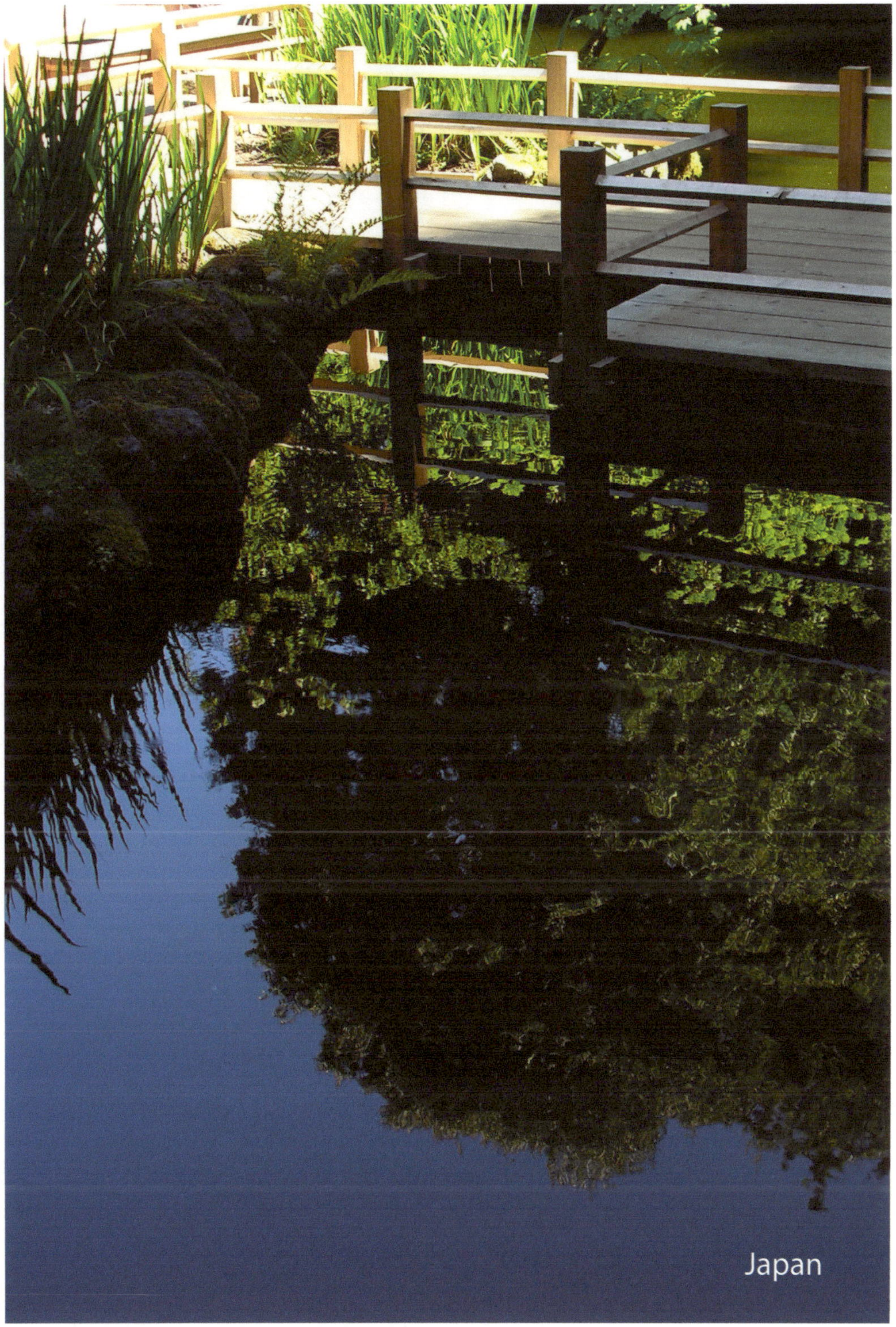

Japan

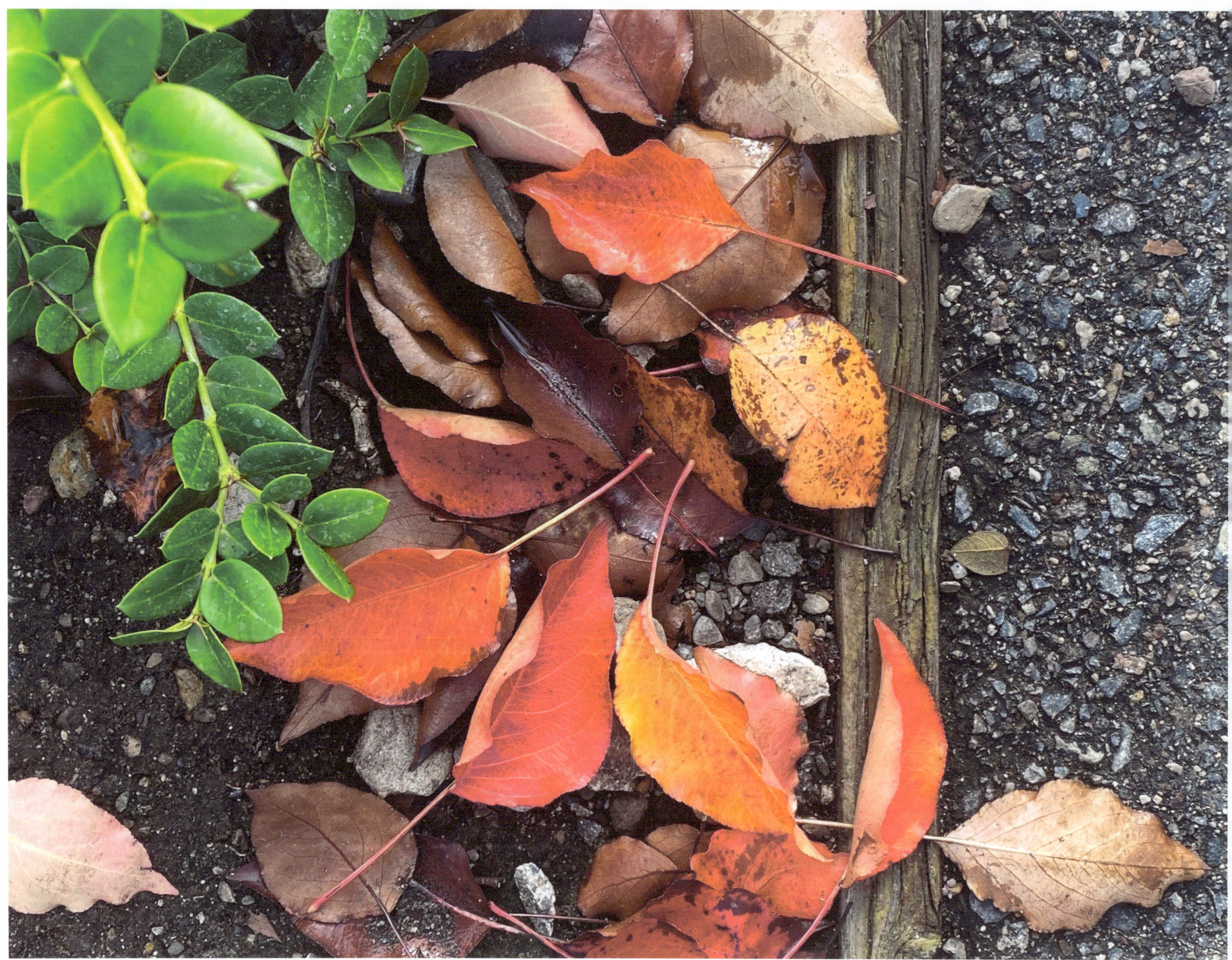

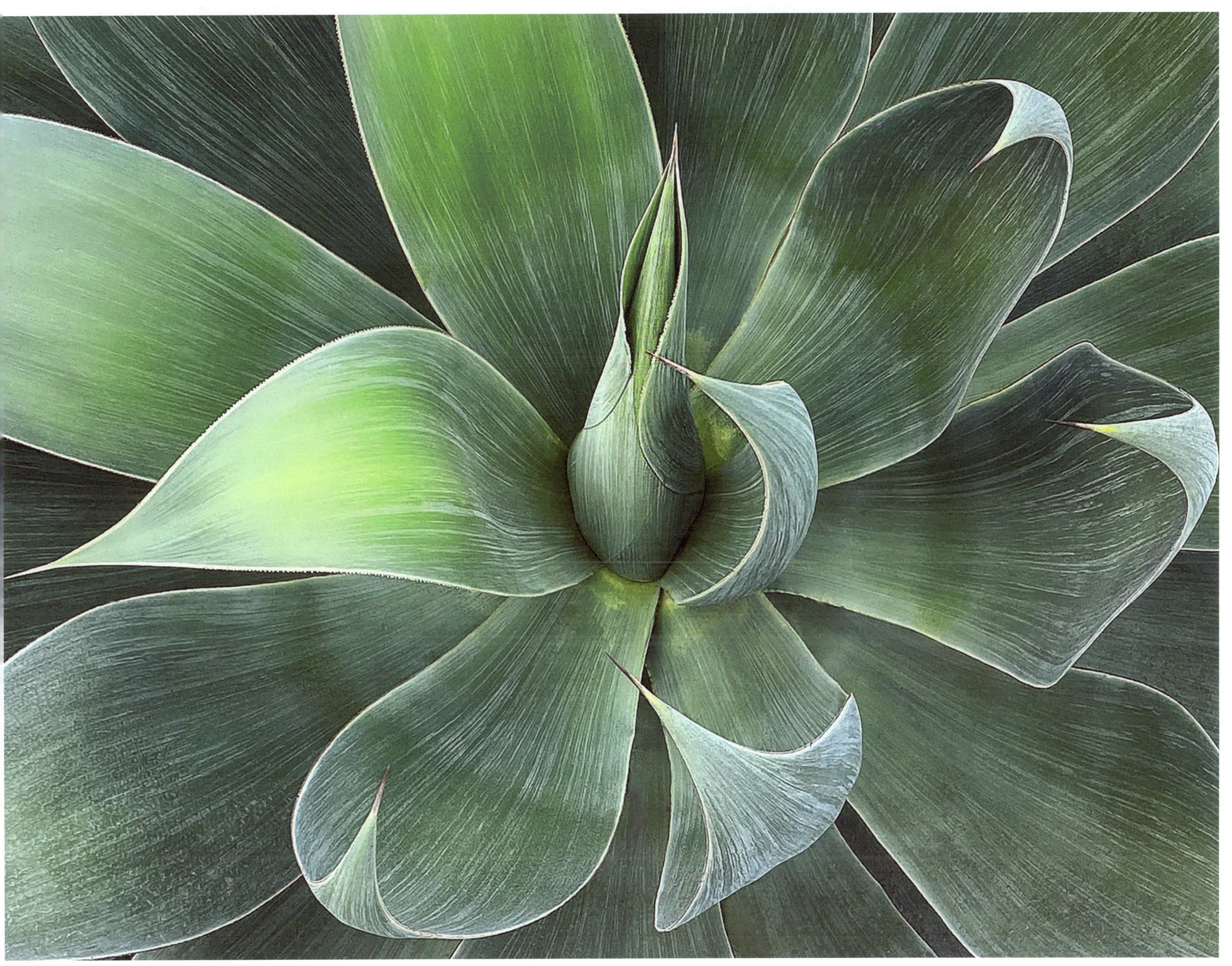

Our landscape focuses on the variety, the nuances of shapes, colors, and lighting that together capture the magnificence of the world around us. Water, air, and climate are temptations for the eye of the camera. The breathtaking Grand Canyon, the power of crashing waves, and the peace of the amber waves of grain are all photographic moments.

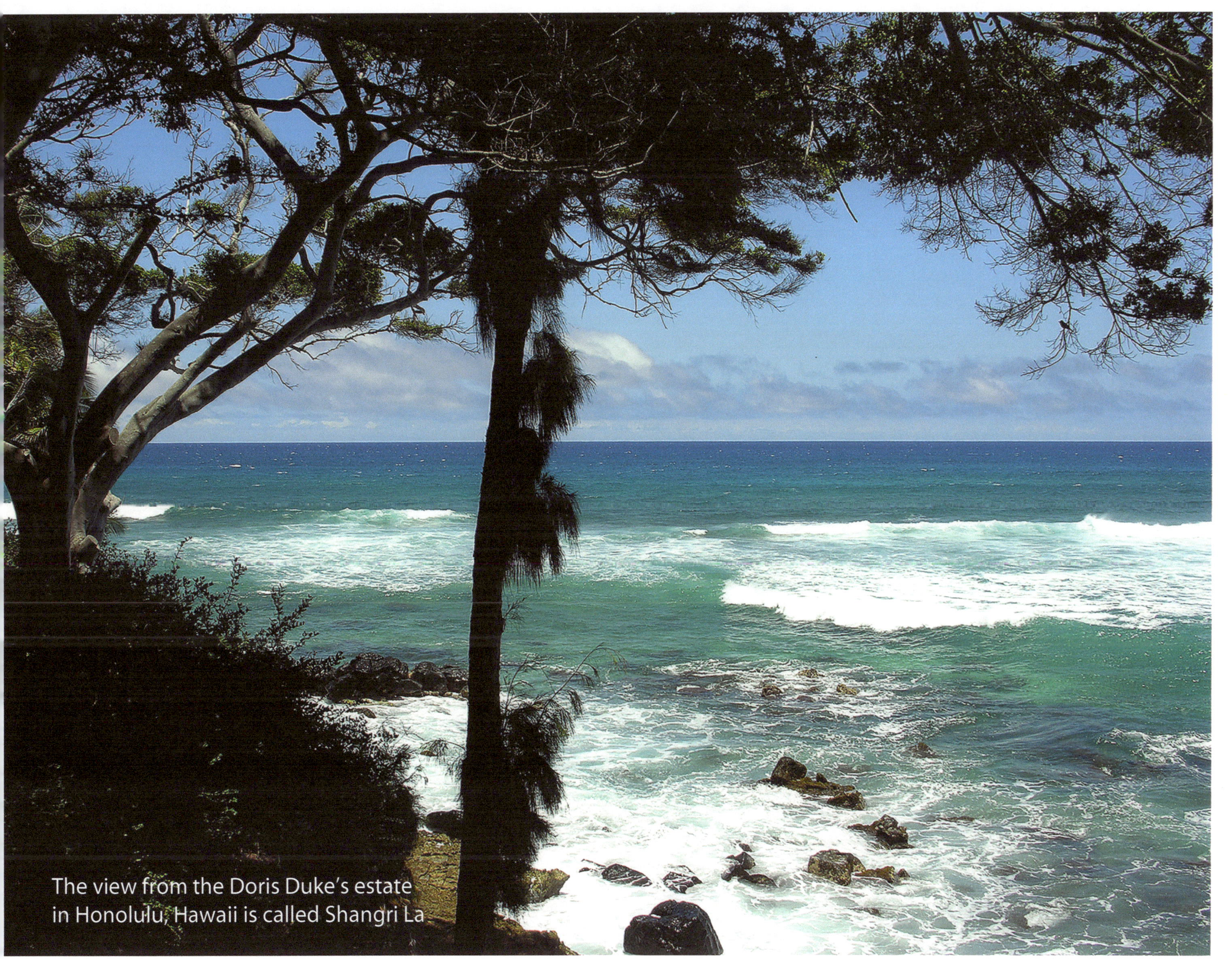

The view from the Doris Duke's estate
in Honolulu, Hawaii is called Shangri La

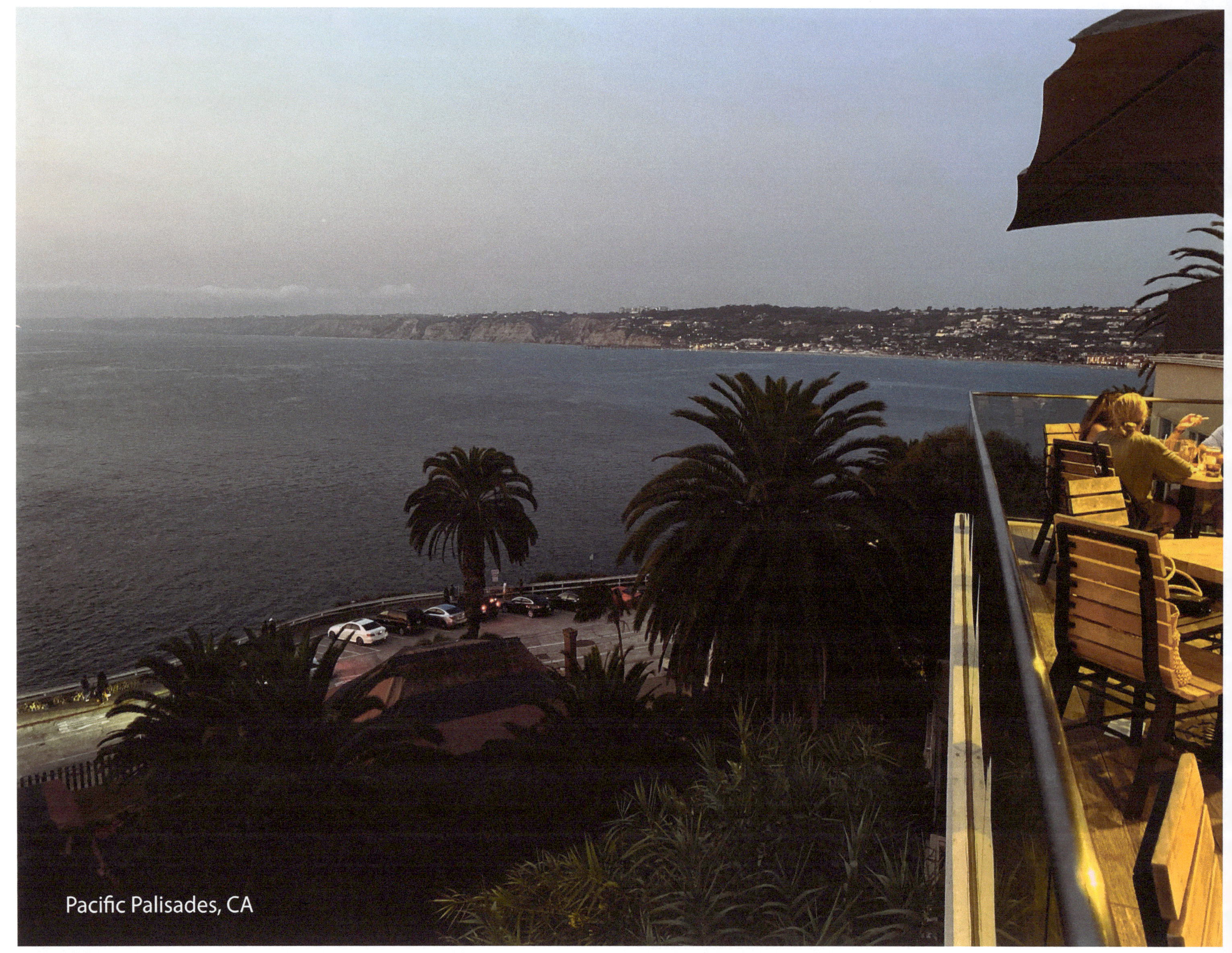
Pacific Palisades, CA

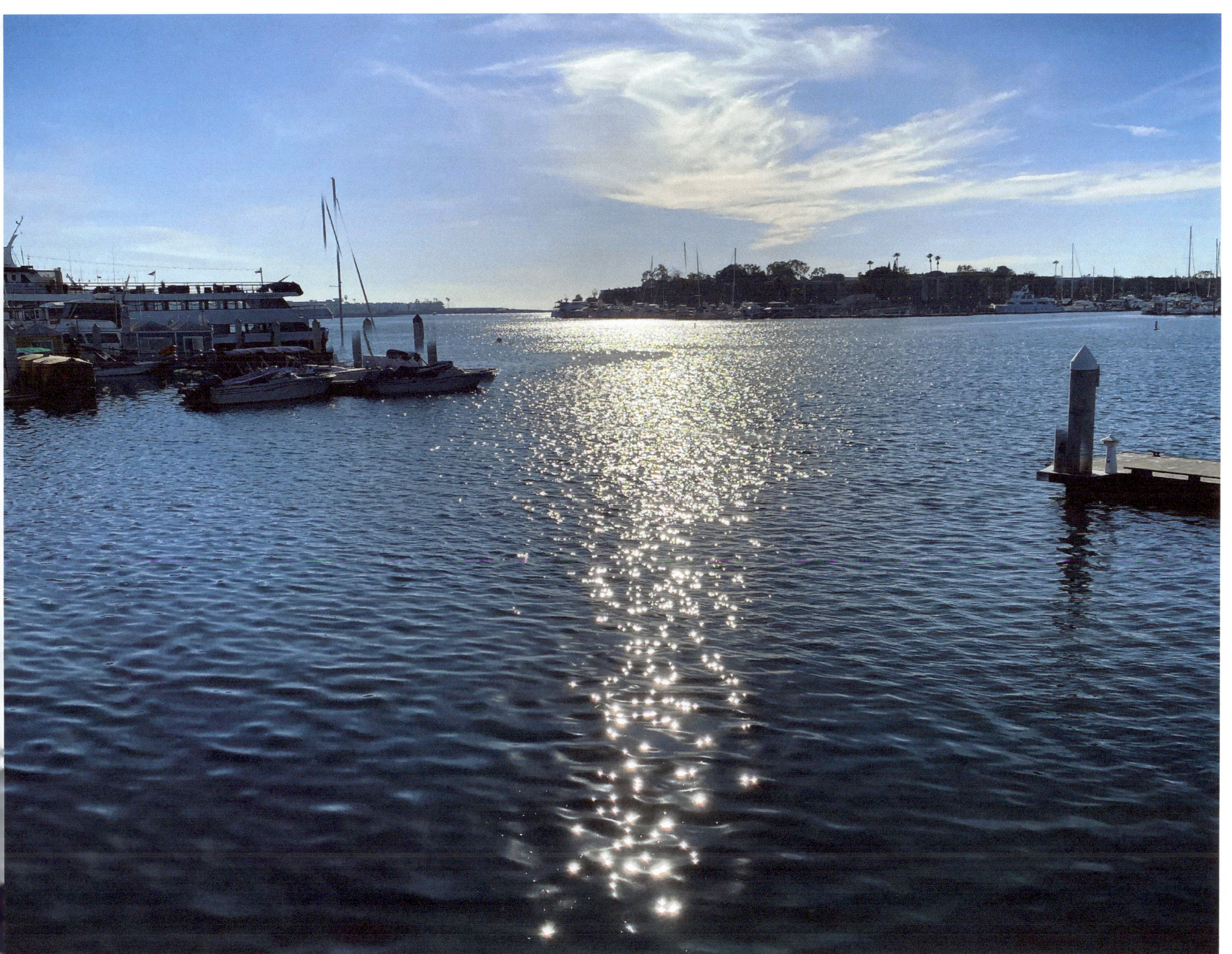

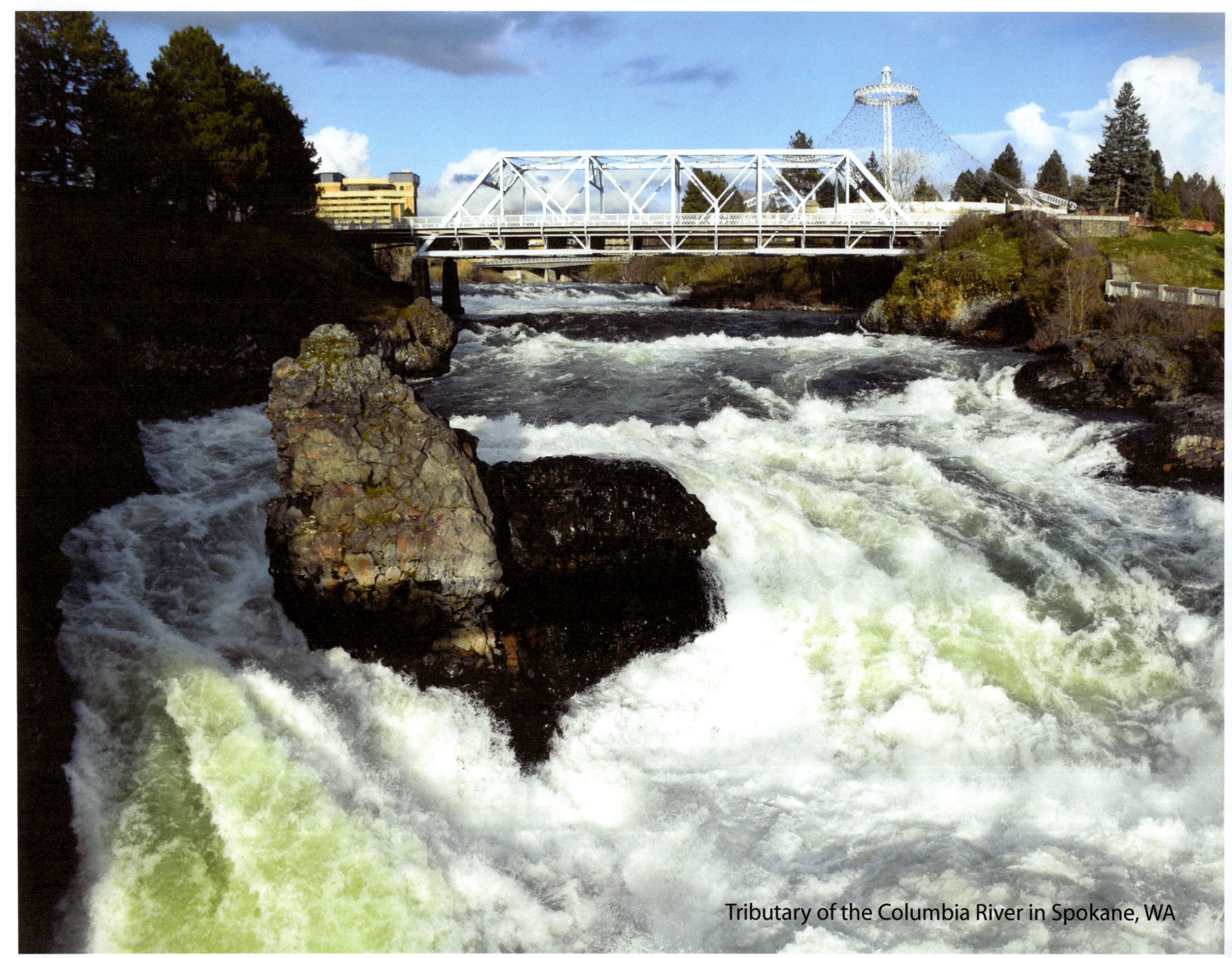
Tributary of the Columbia River in Spokane, WA

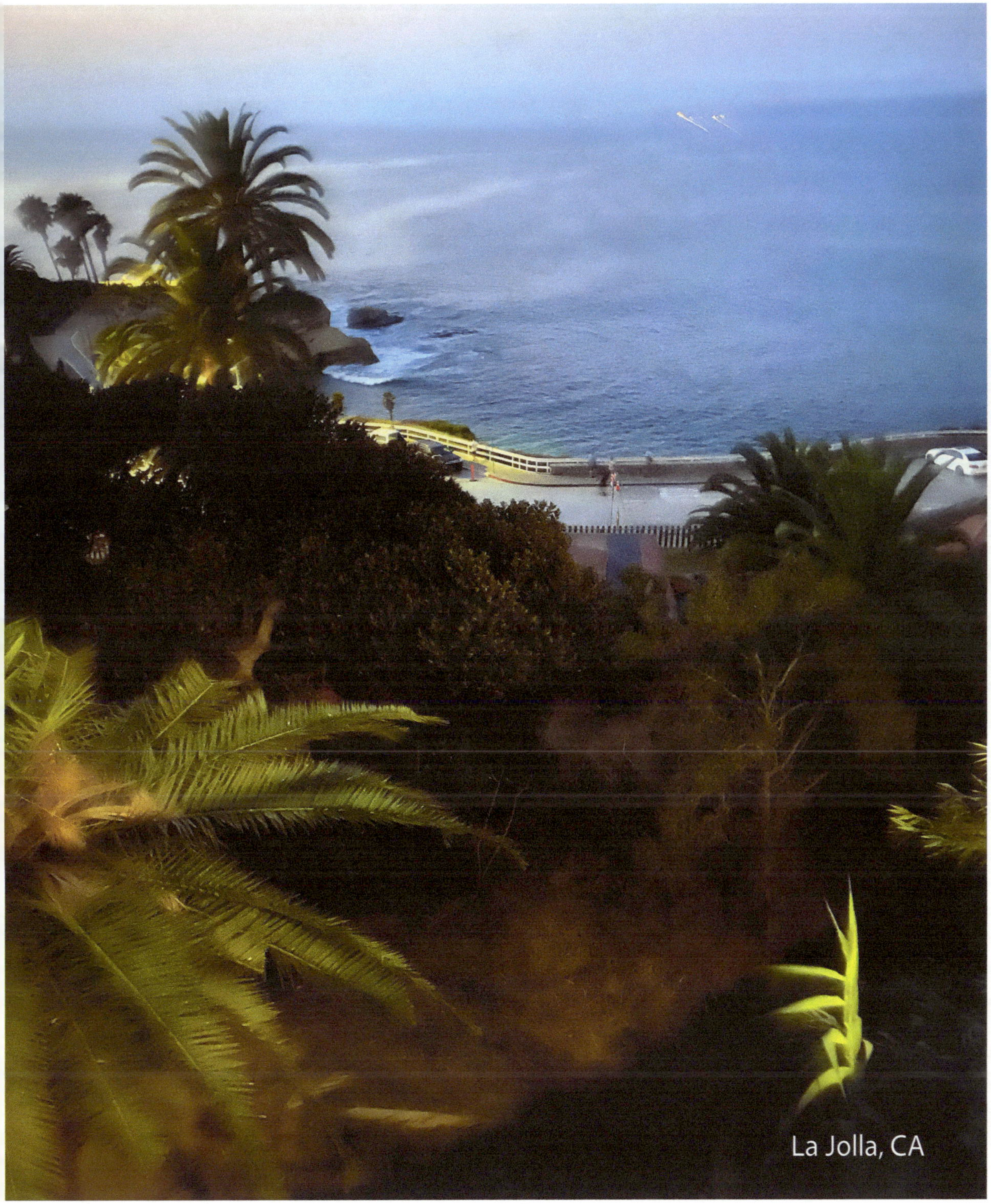

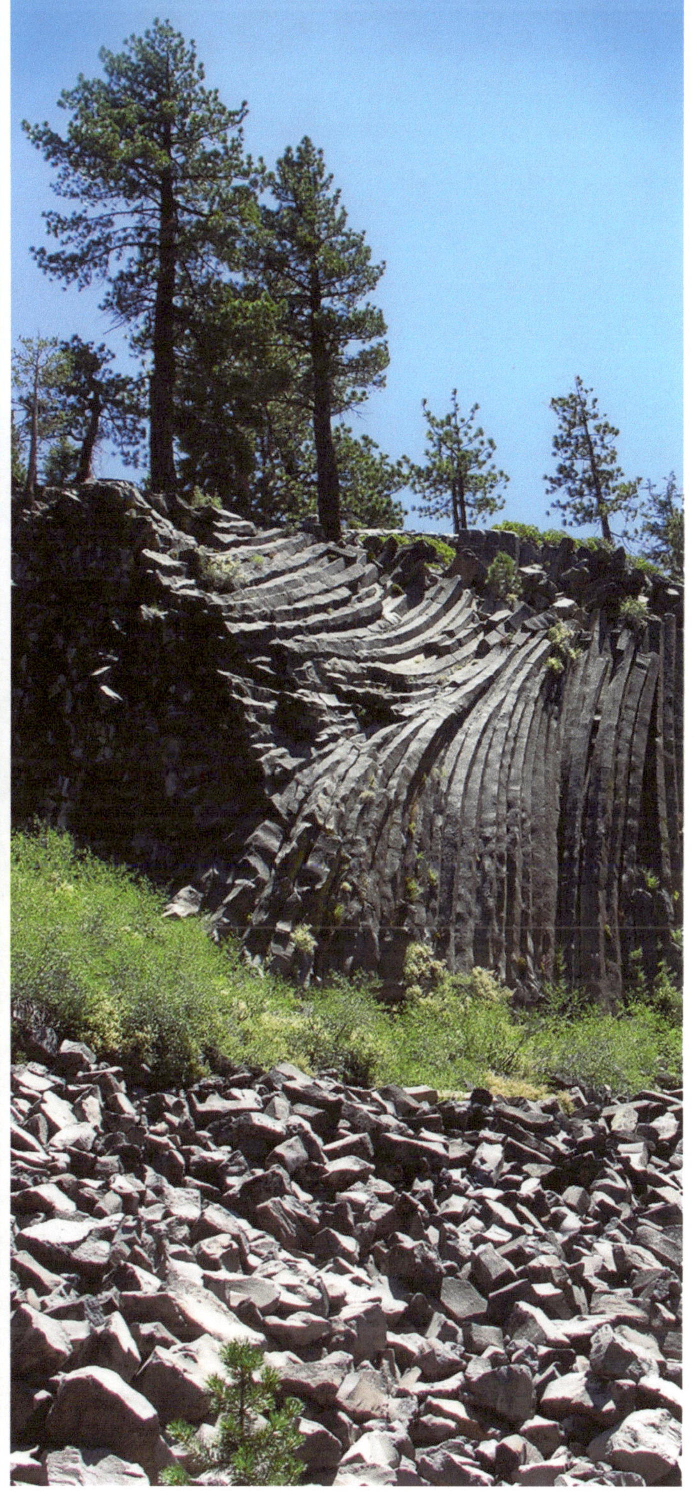

La Jolla, CA

Photography captures and historically records the sheer wonder of man's creativity in the creation of the infrastructure necessary for humanity. Not only dwellings, skyscrapers, bridges, highways, but also all the many other elements that complete these structures. They shelter, protect, functionally comfort us, as well as wrap us aesthetically.

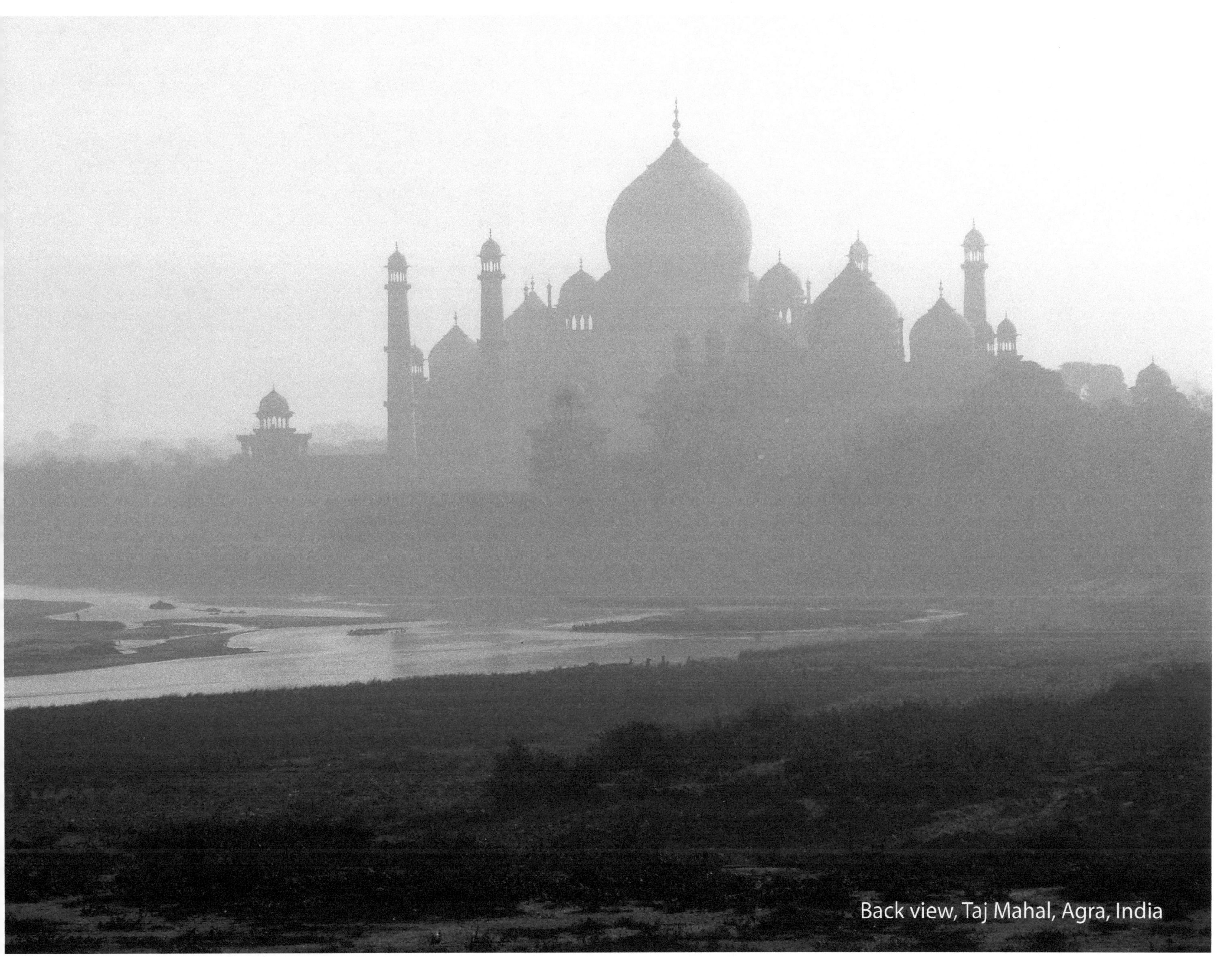

Back view, Taj Mahal, Agra, India

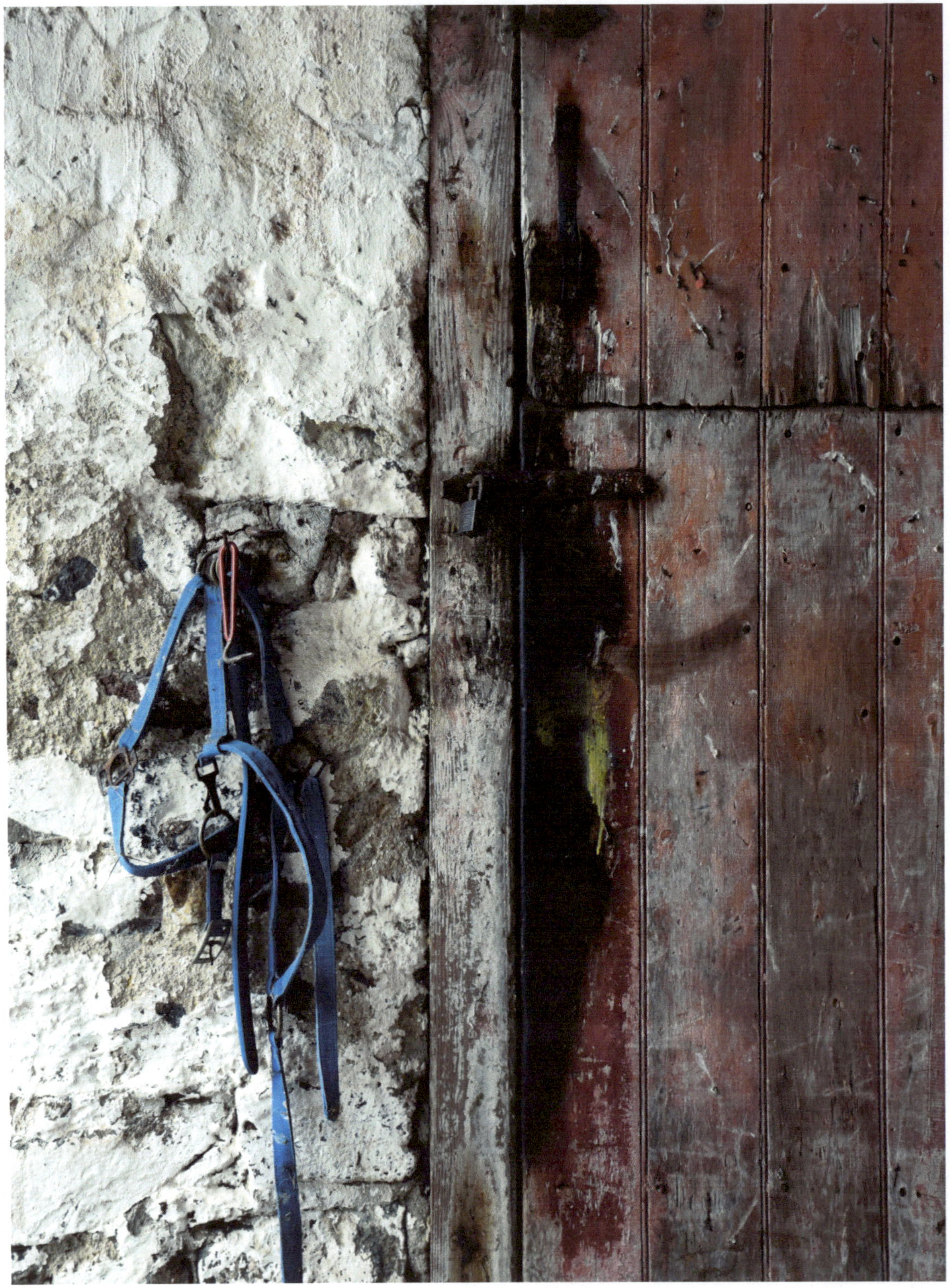

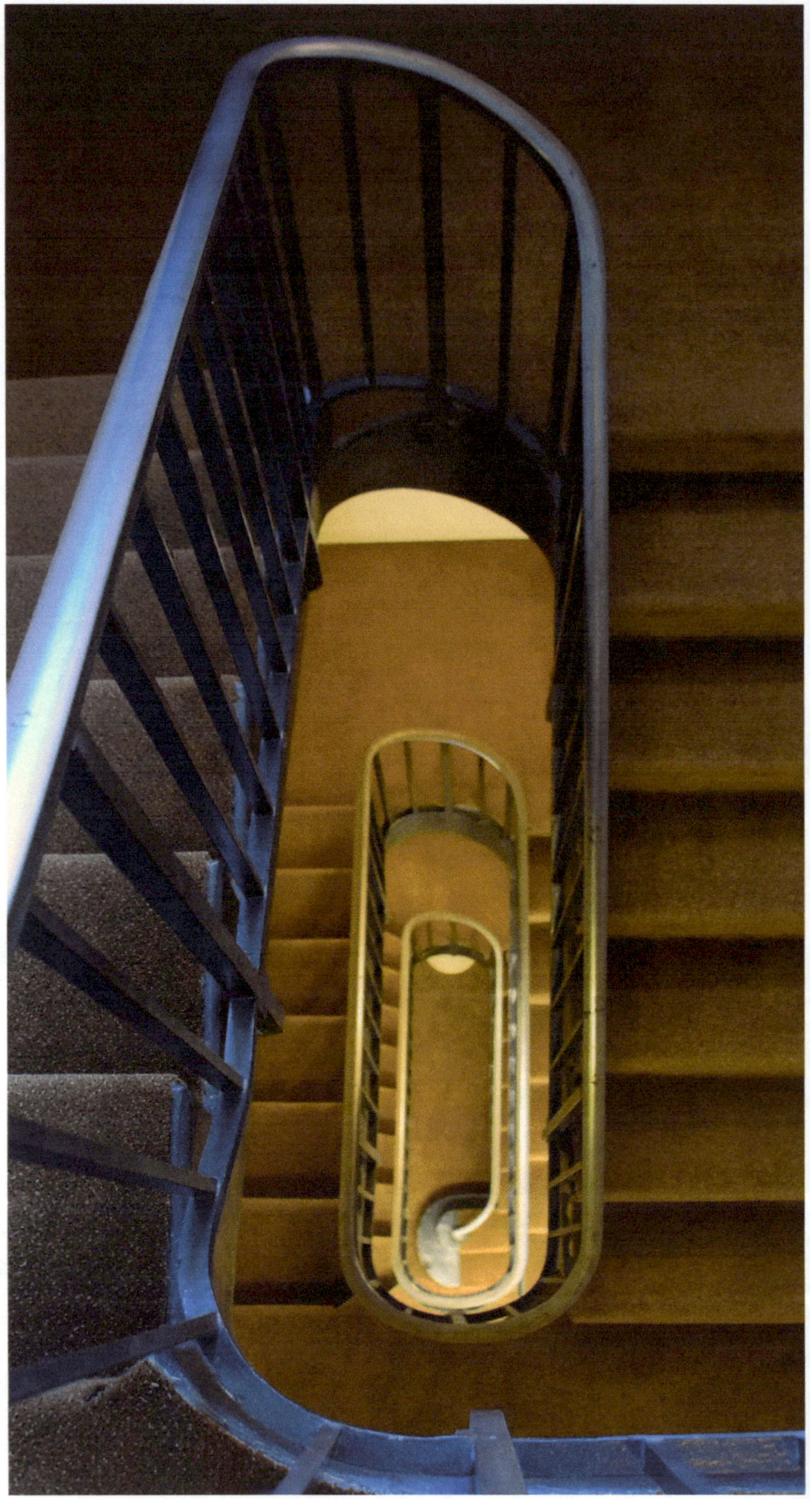

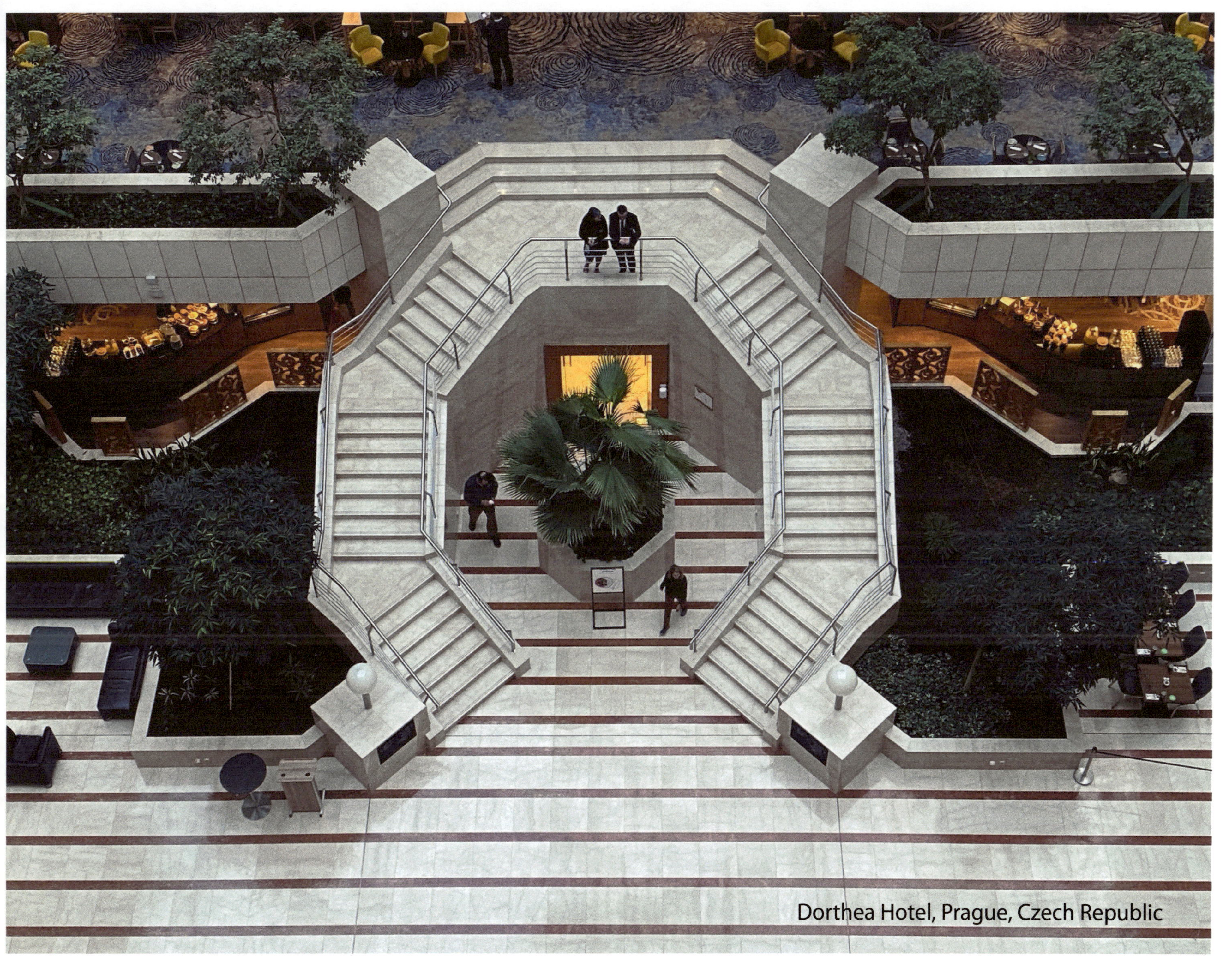

Dorthea Hotel, Prague, Czech Republic

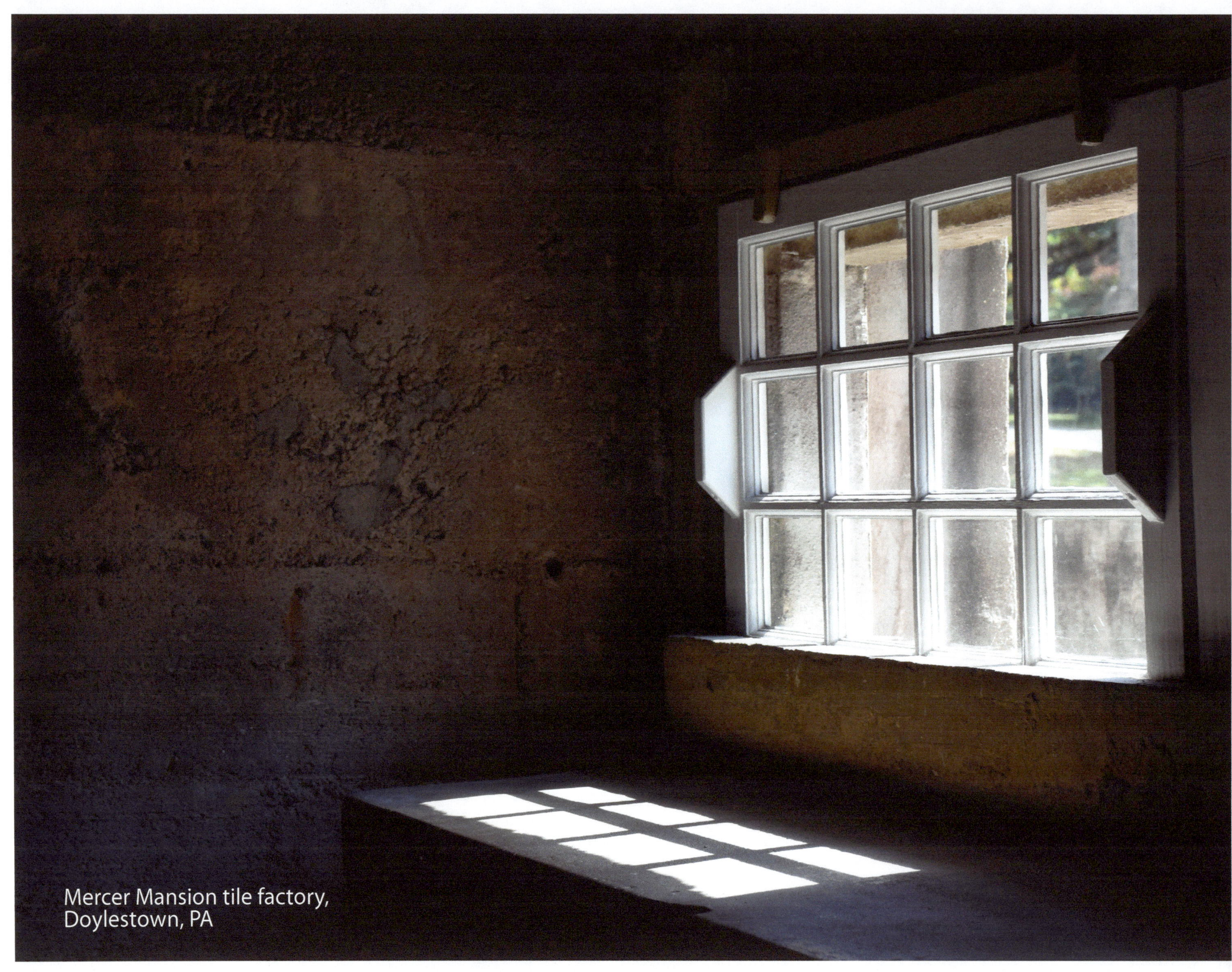

Mercer Mansion tile factory,
Doylestown, PA

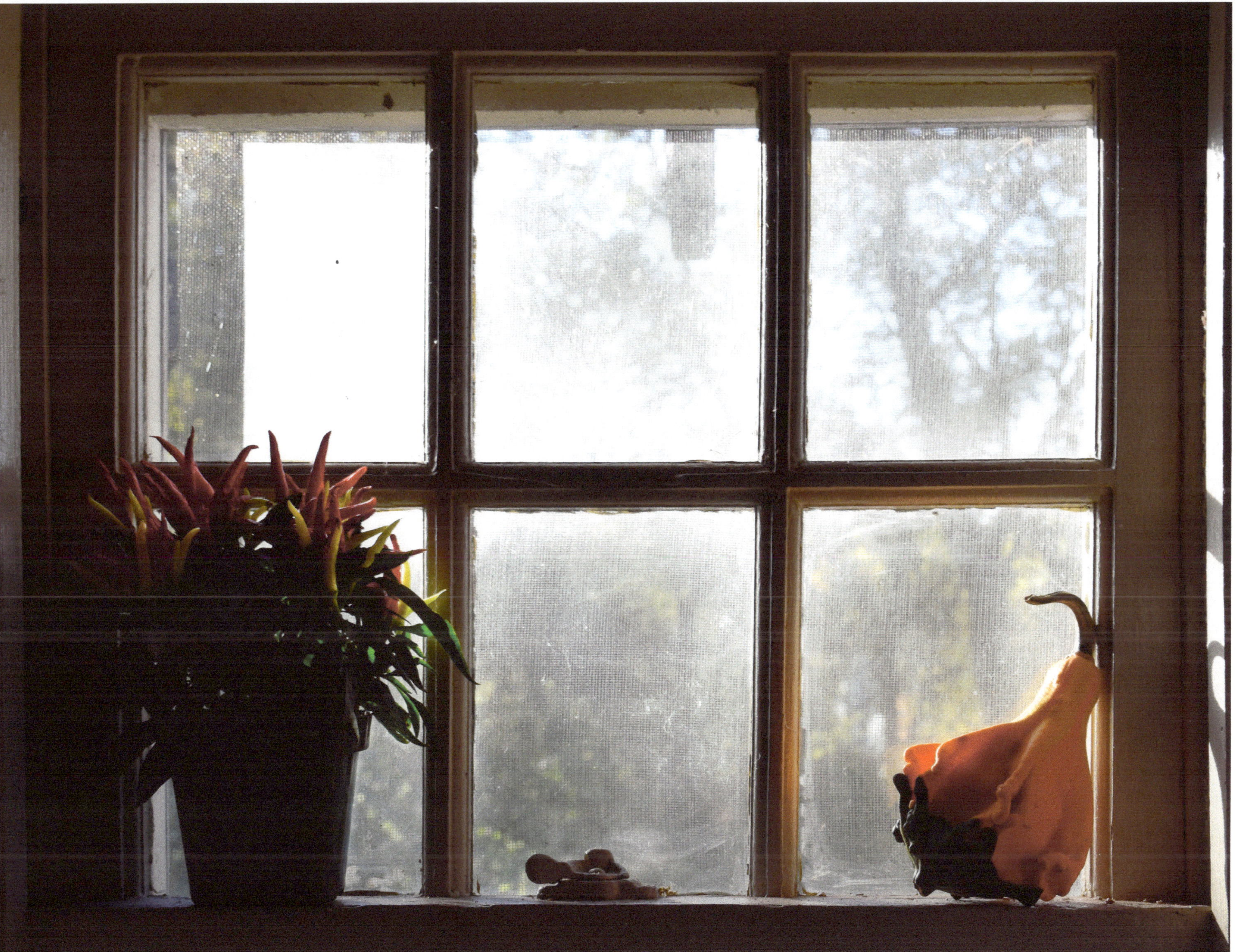

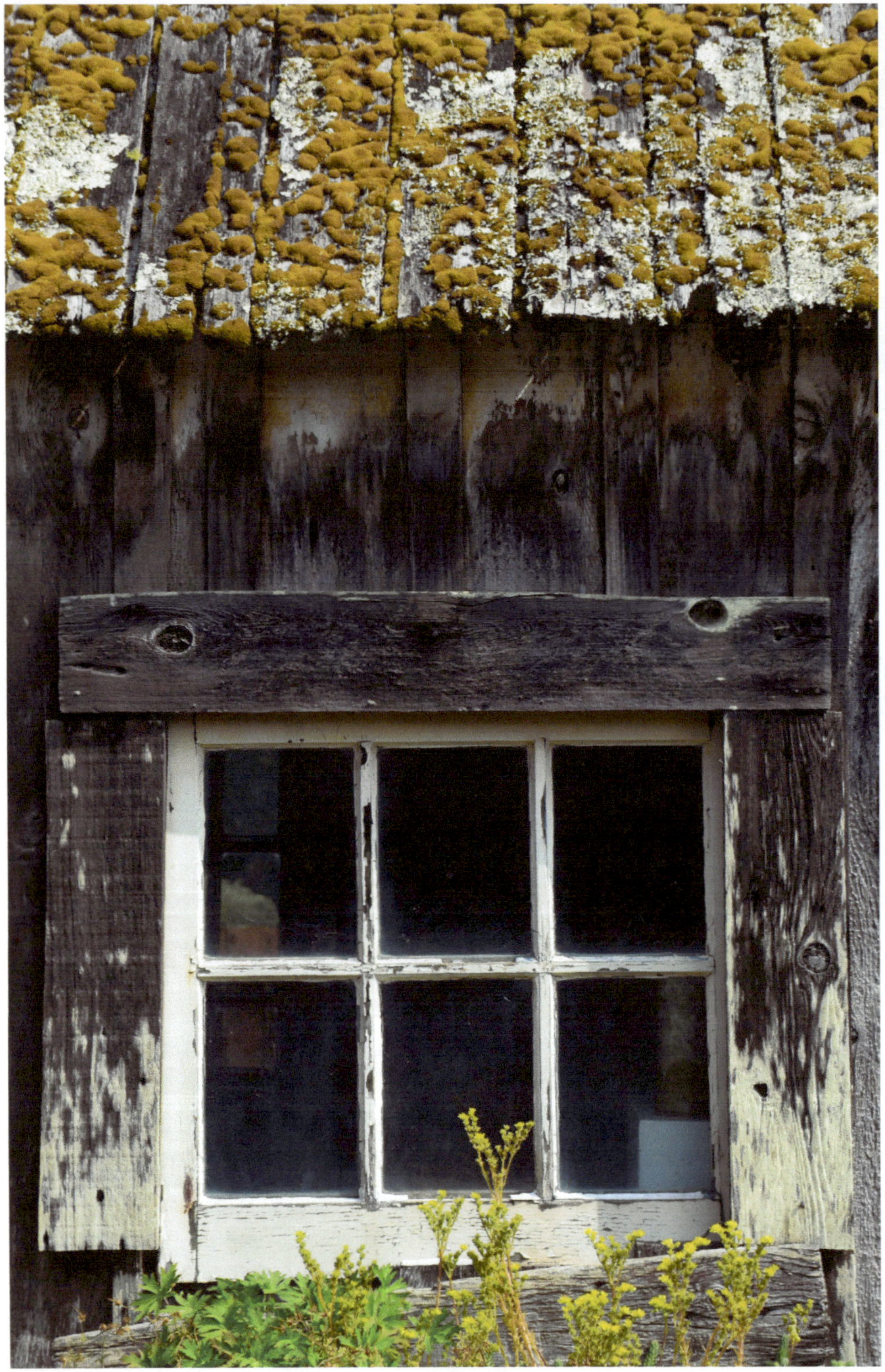

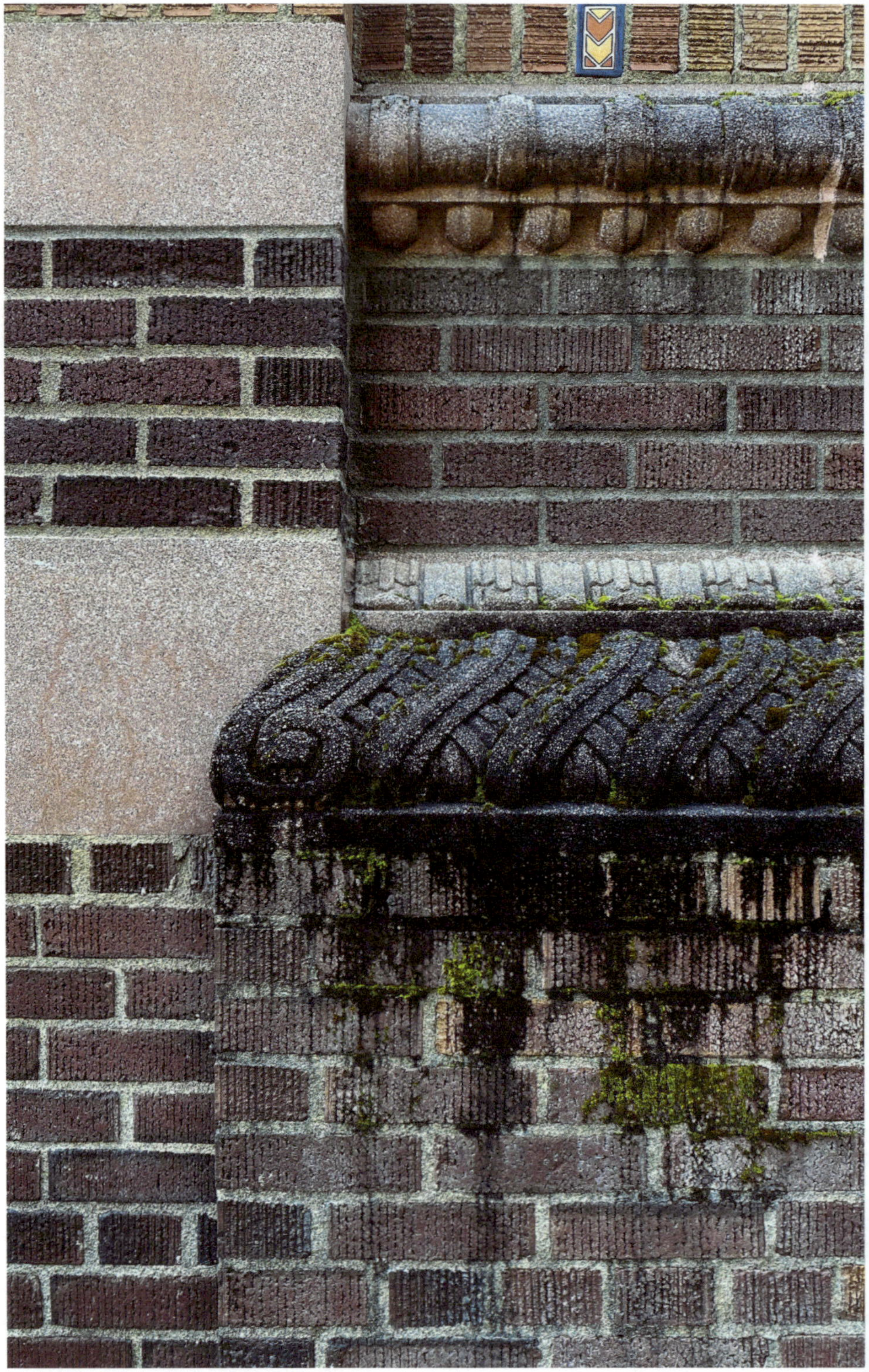

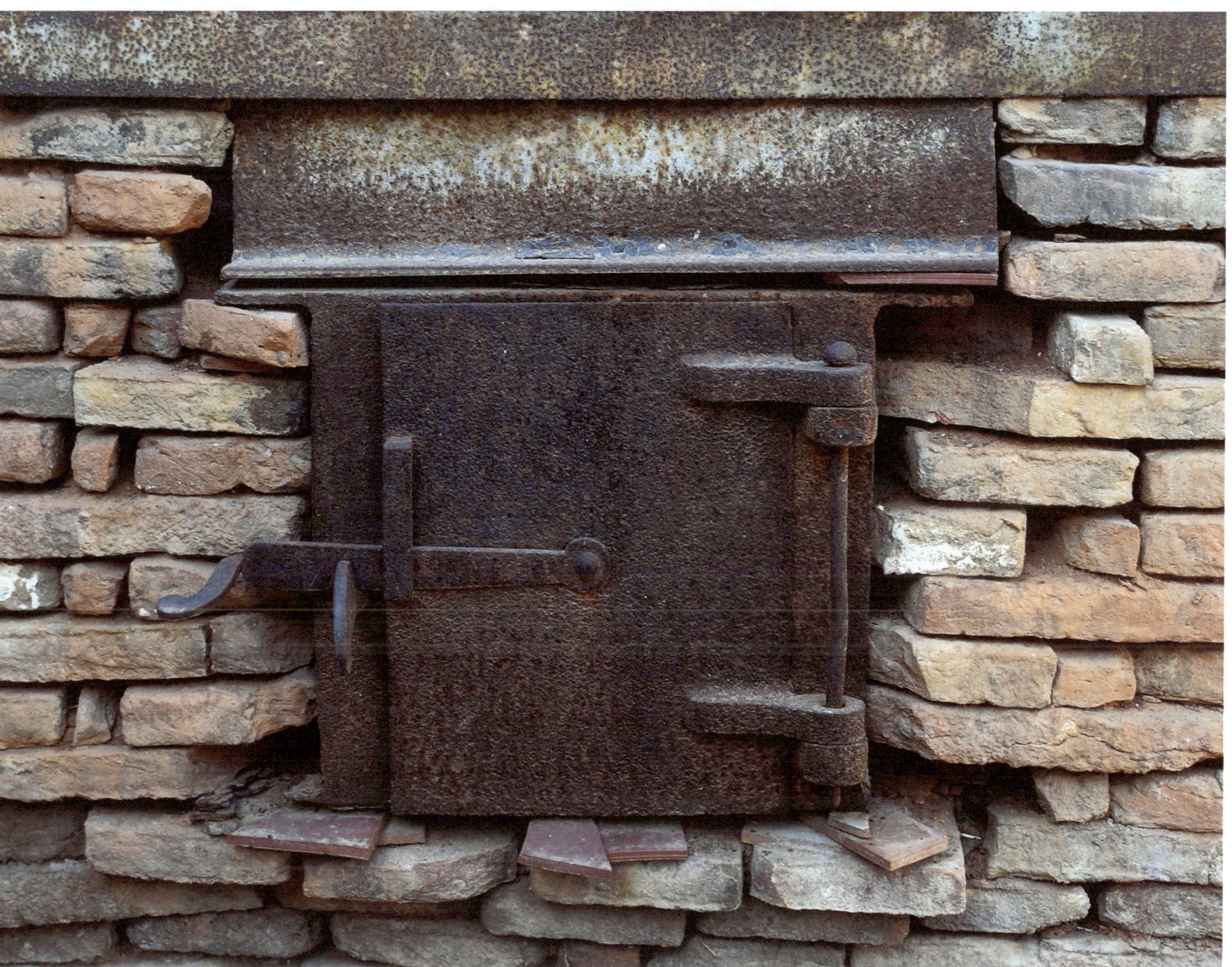

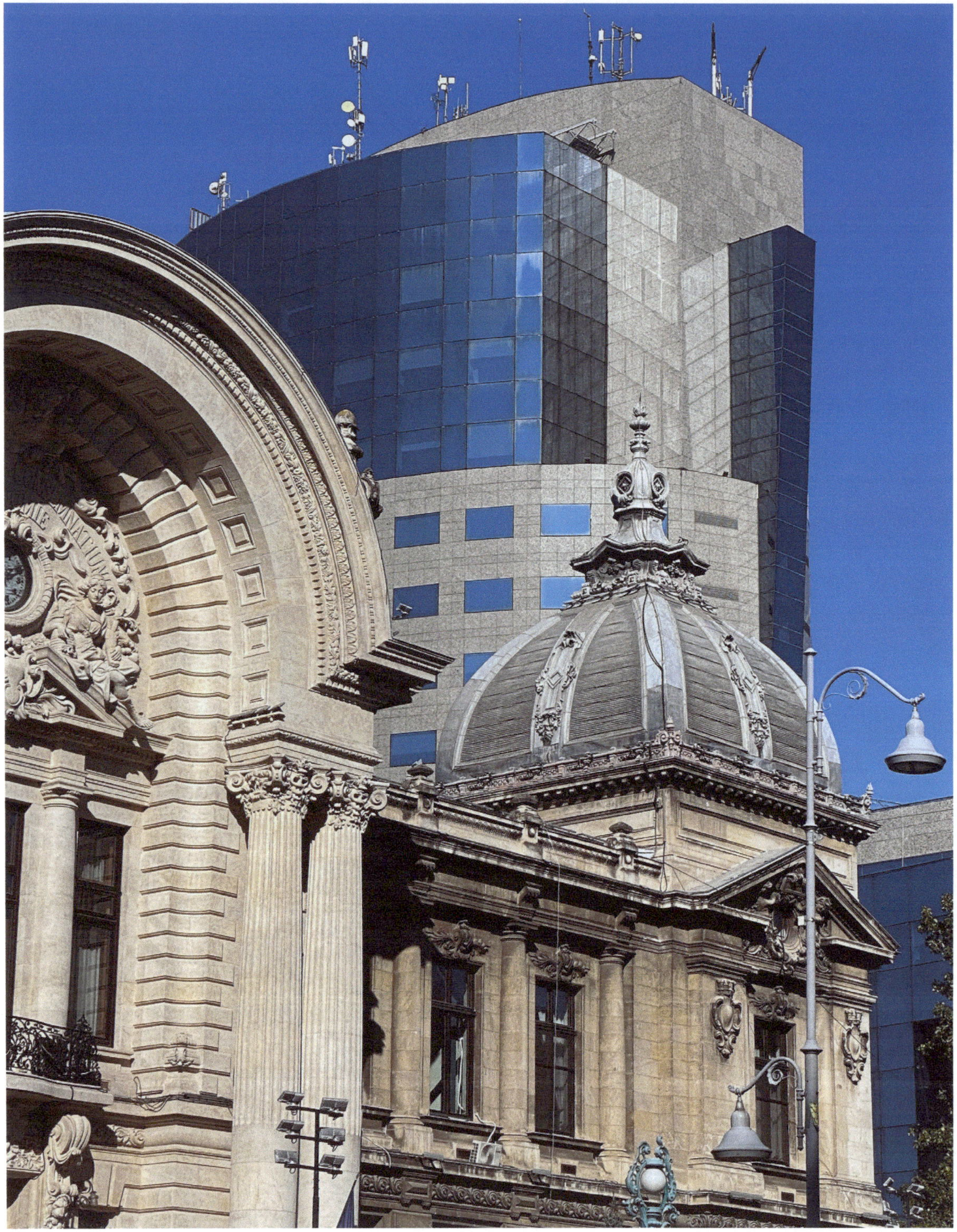

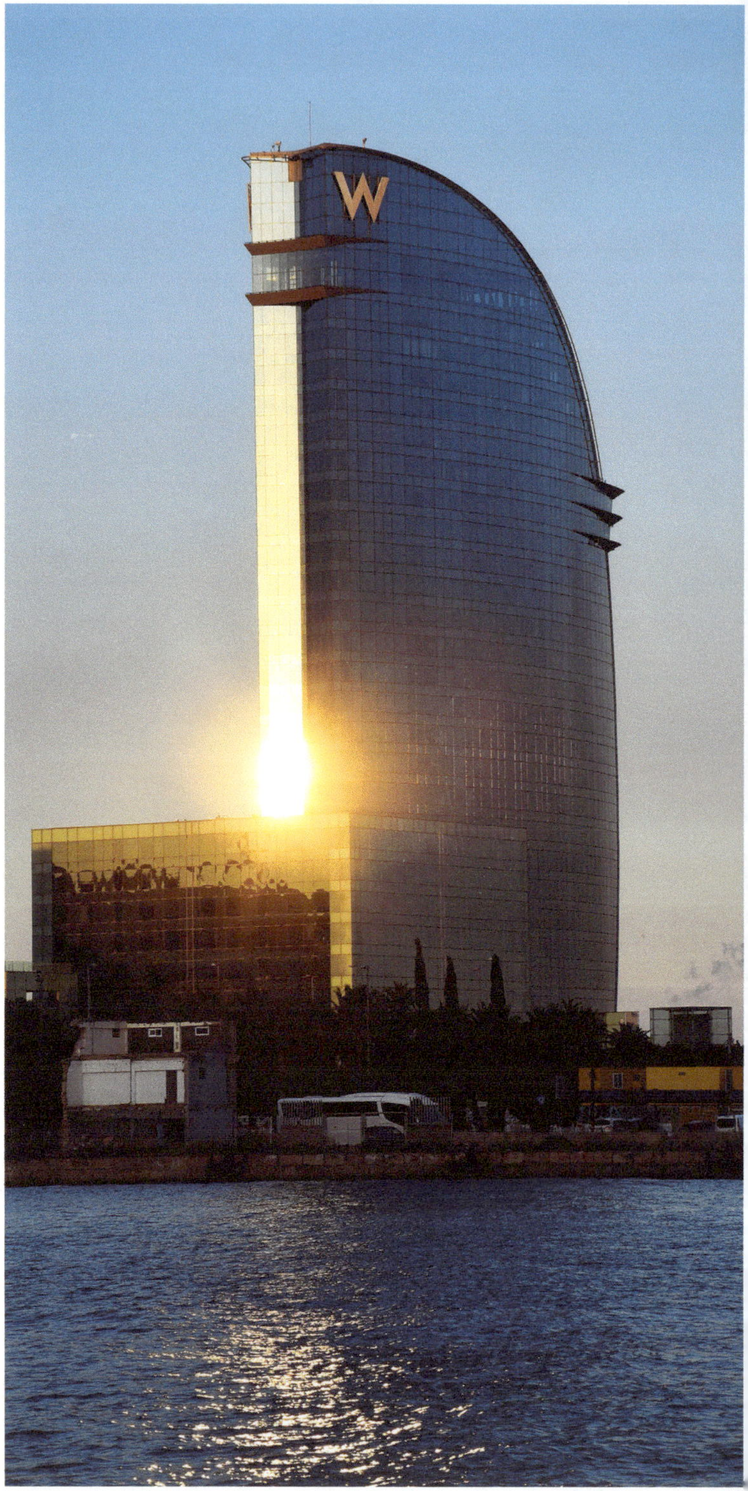

W

*Photography is a way of feeling,
of touching, of loving.
What you have caught on film
is captured forever...
It remembers little things,
long after you have forgotten everything.*

\- Aaron Siskind

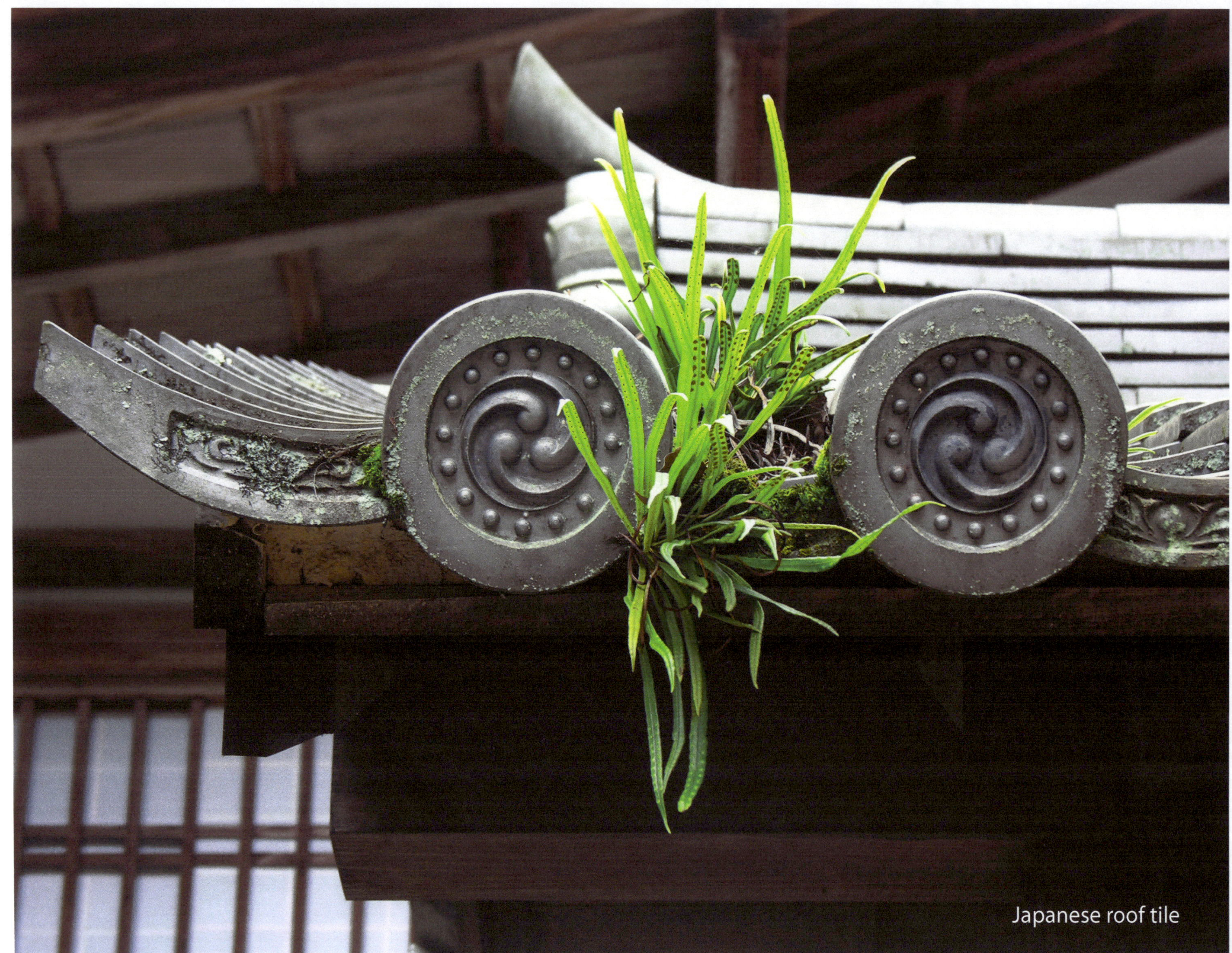

Japanese roof tile

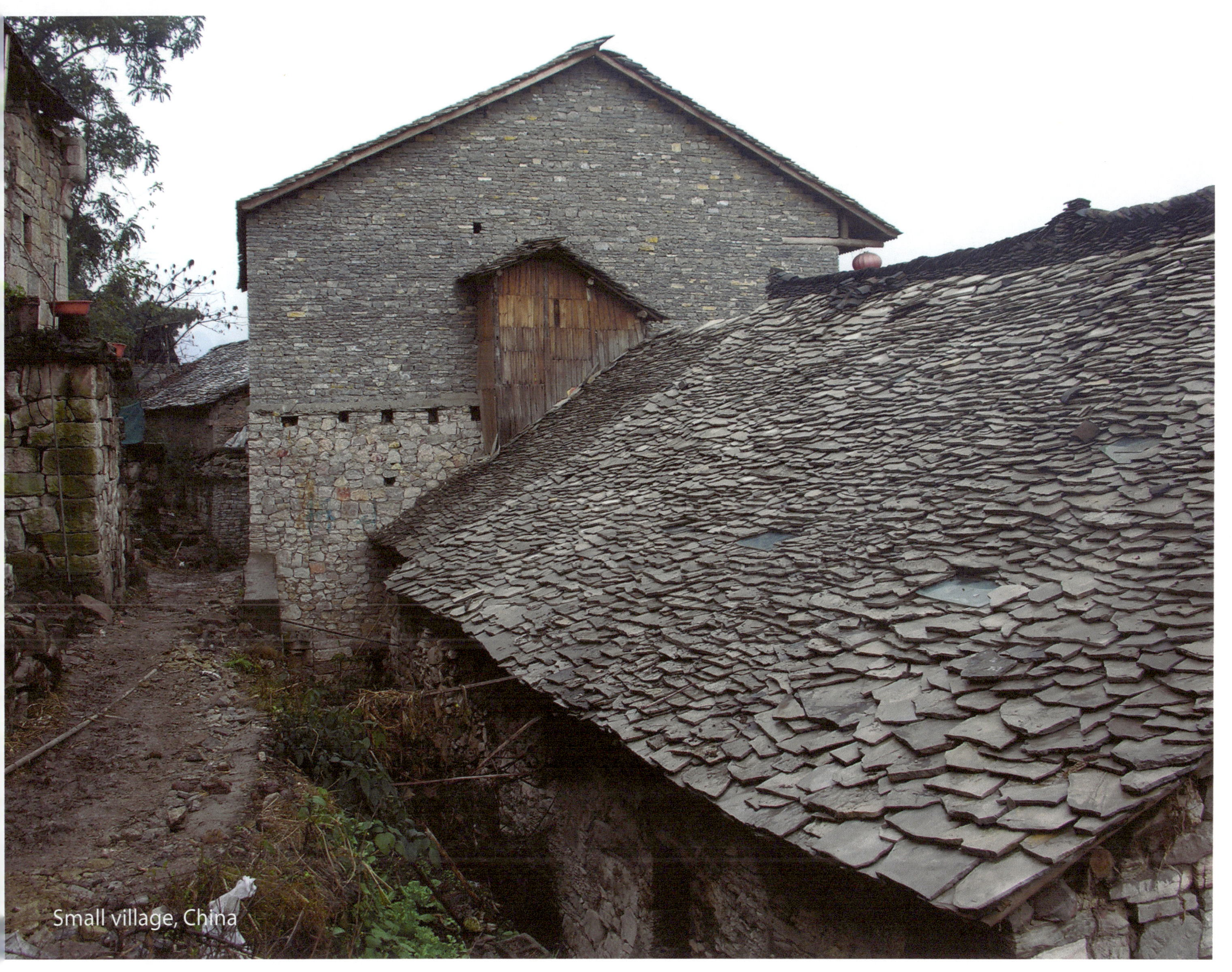

Small village, China

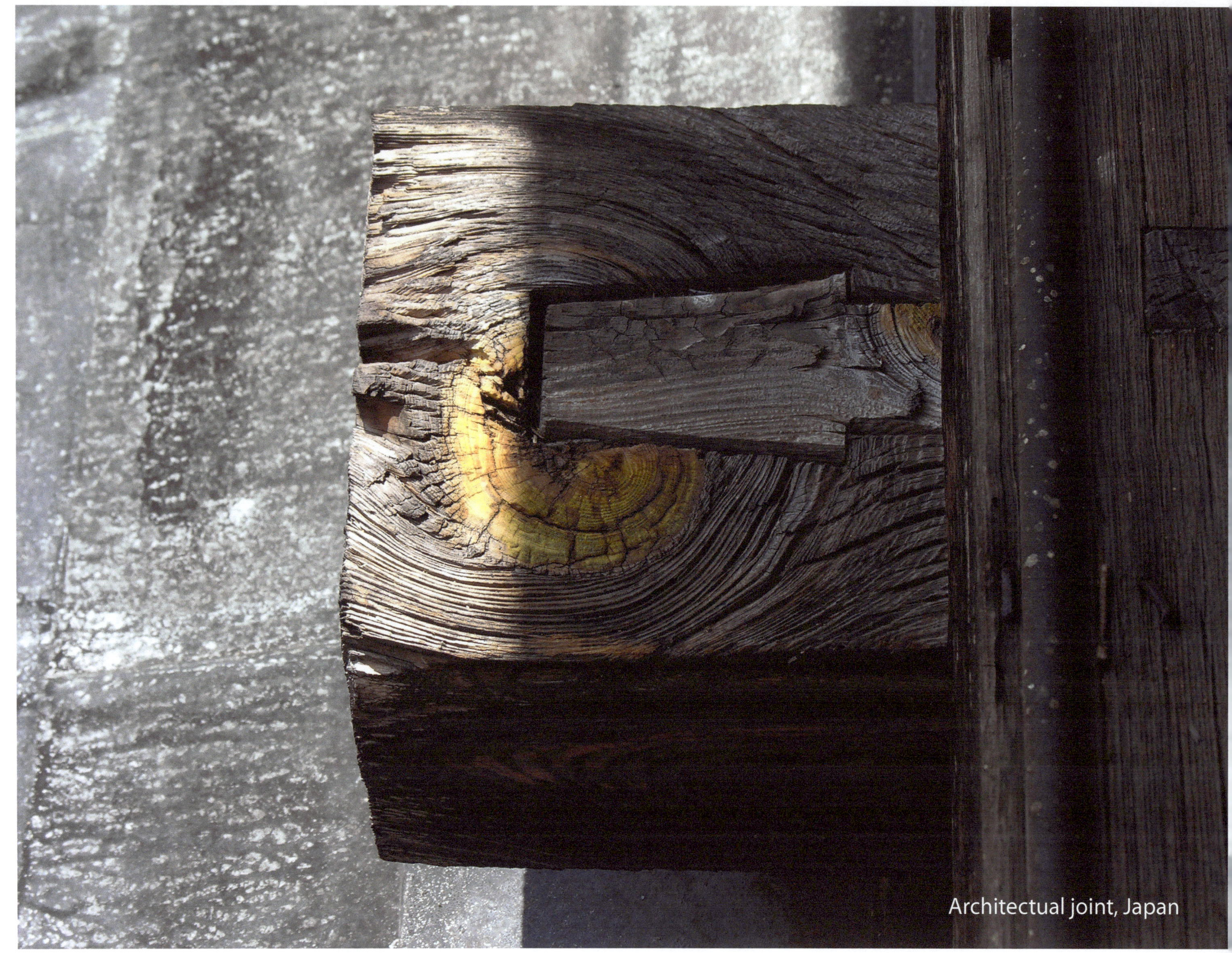

Architectual joint, Japan

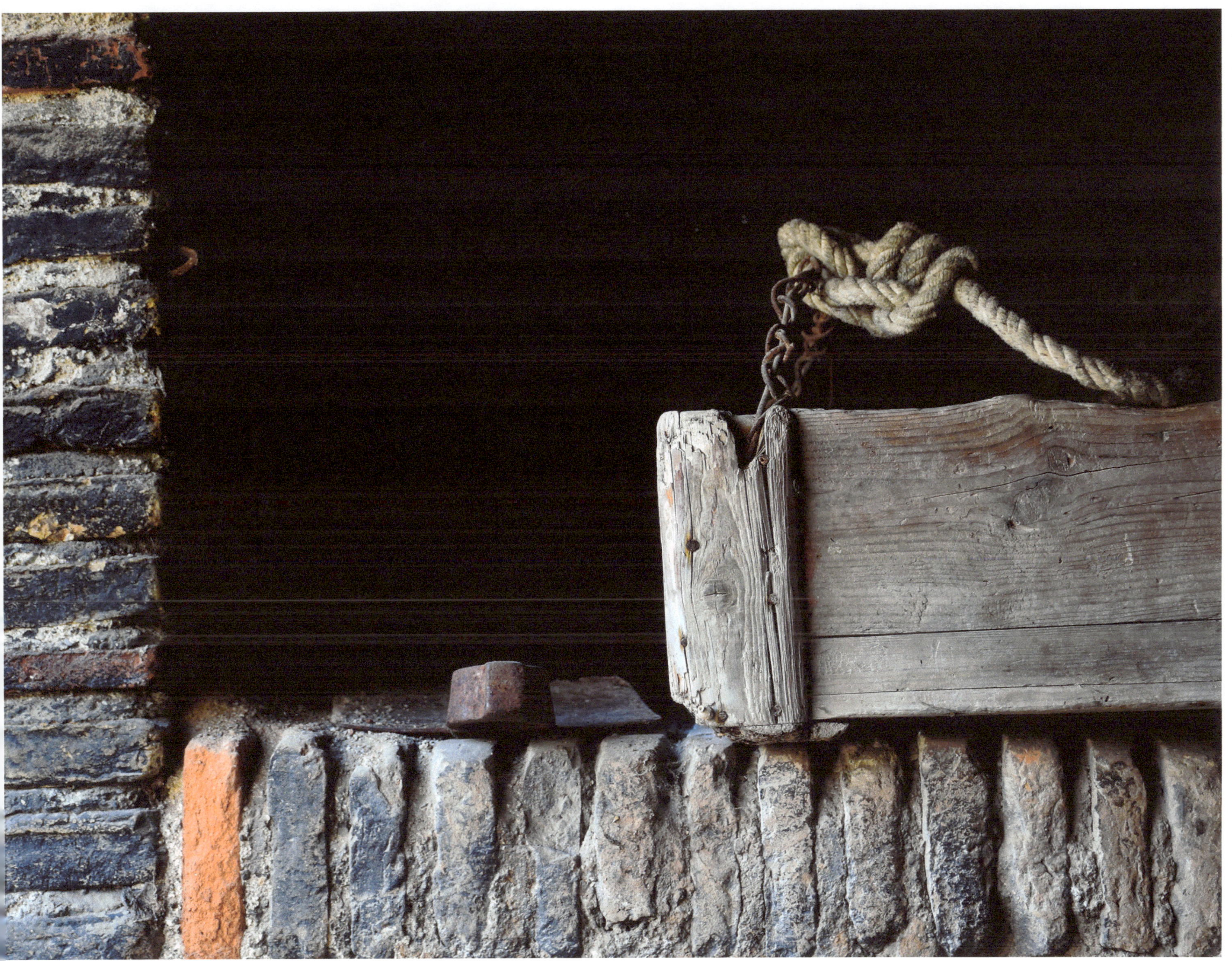

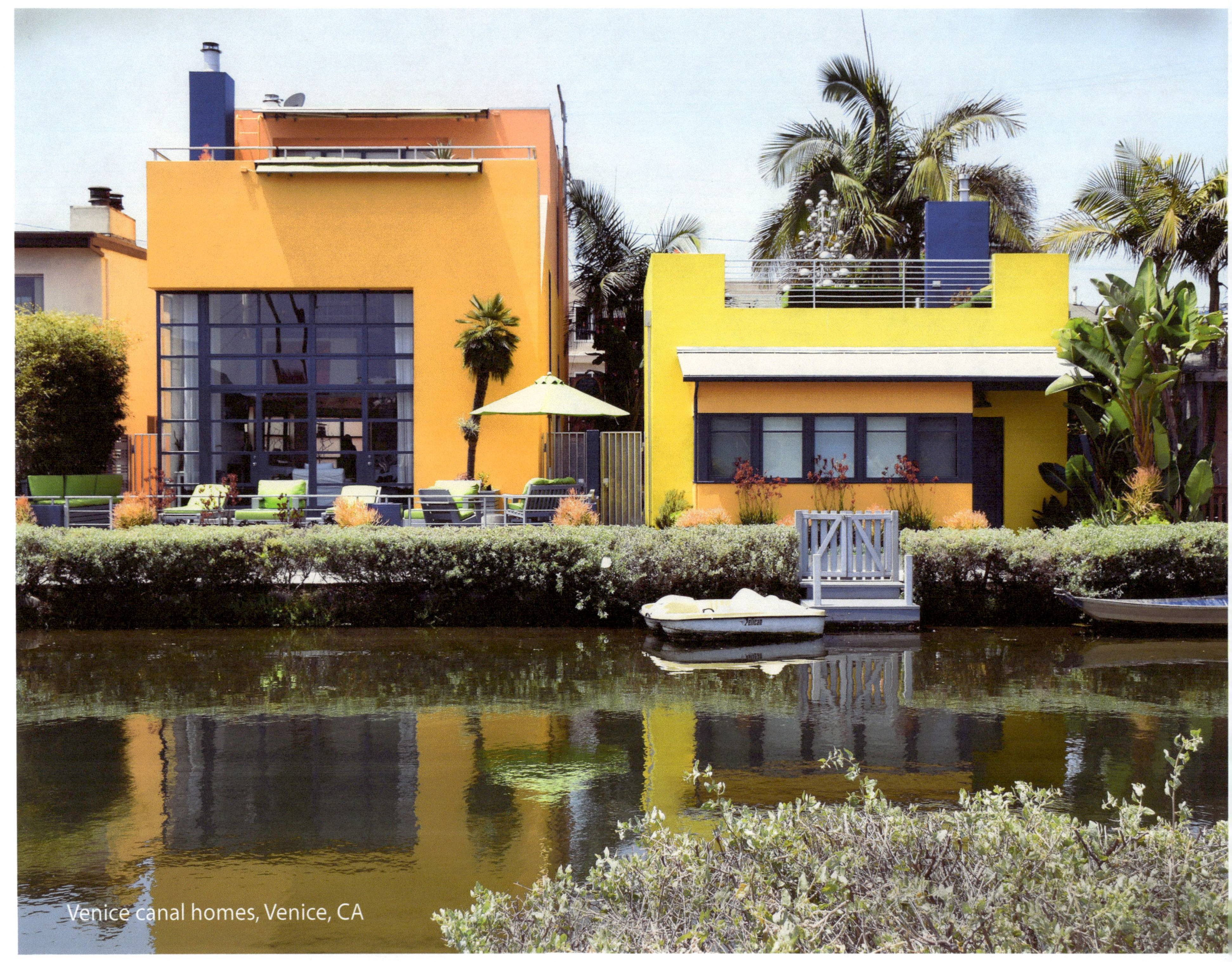

Venice canal homes, Venice, CA

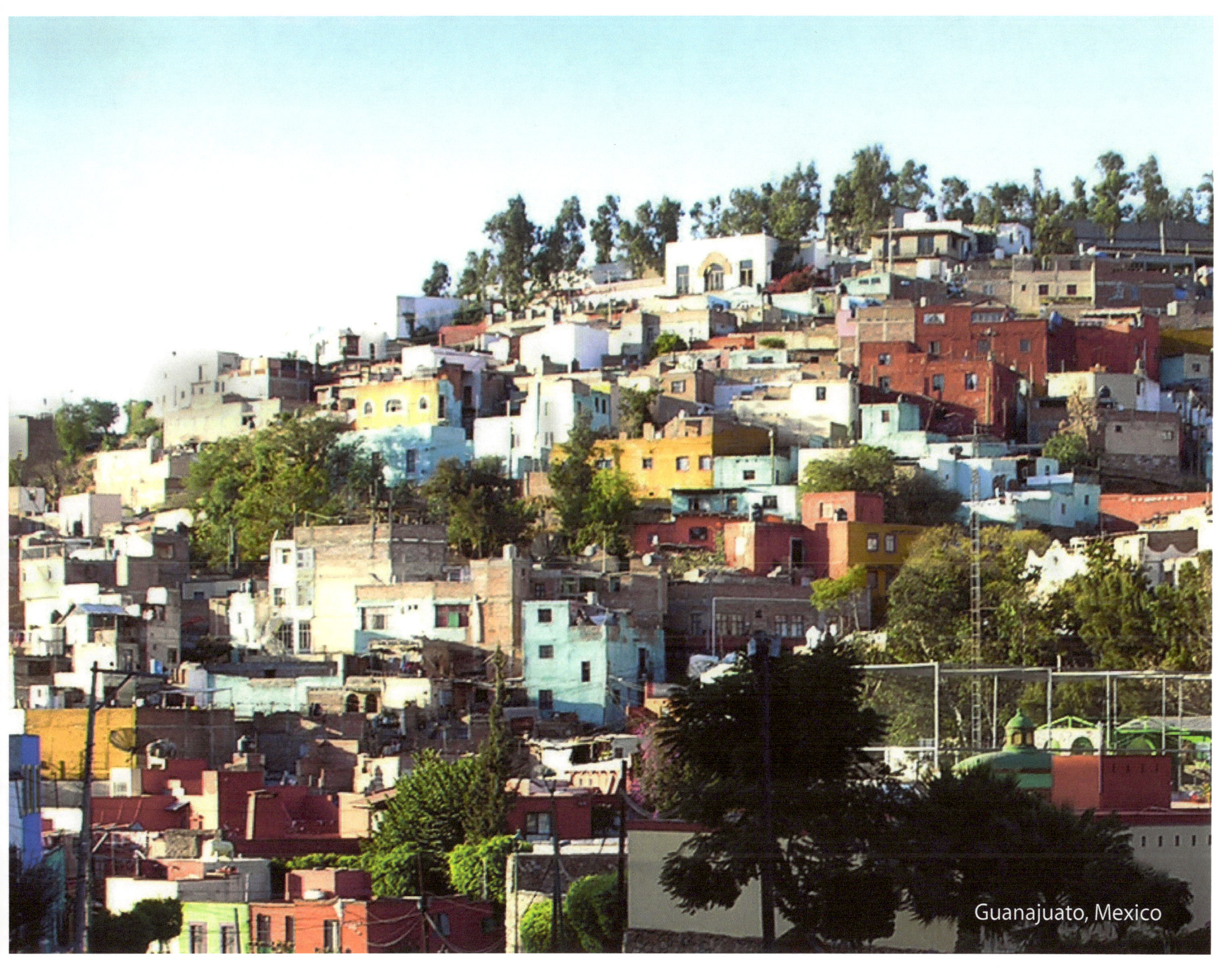
Guanajuato, Mexico

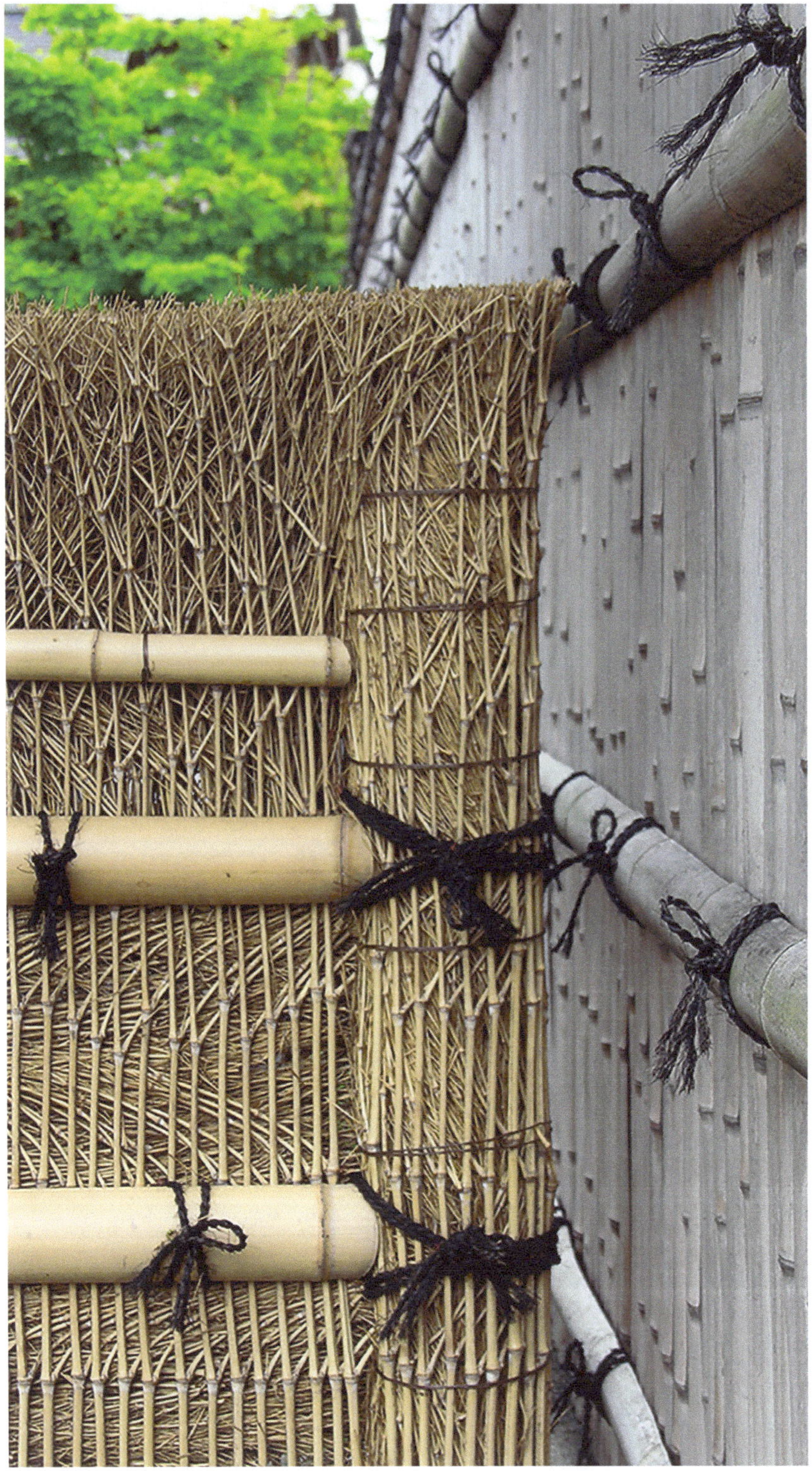

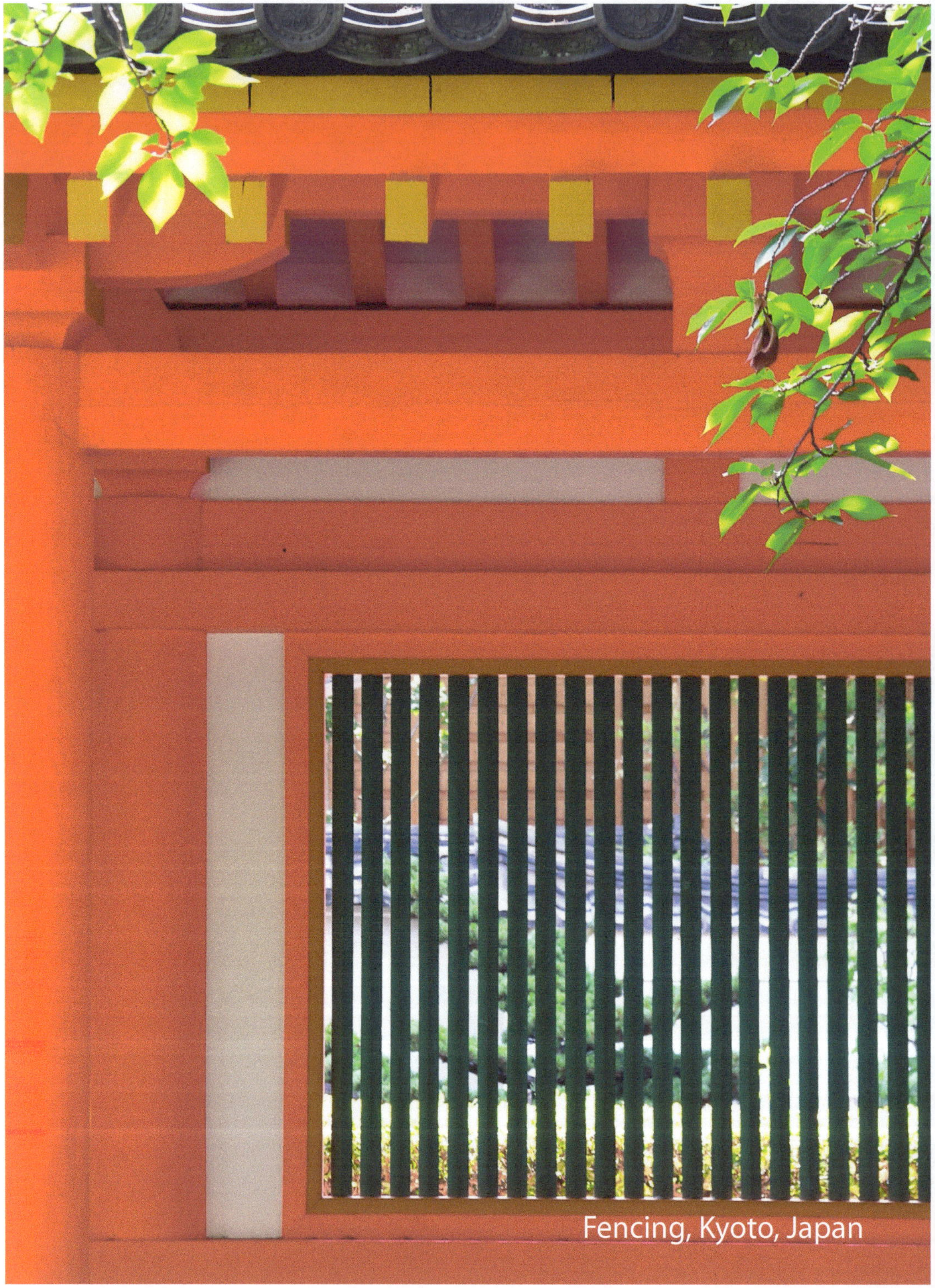

Fencing, Kyoto, Japan

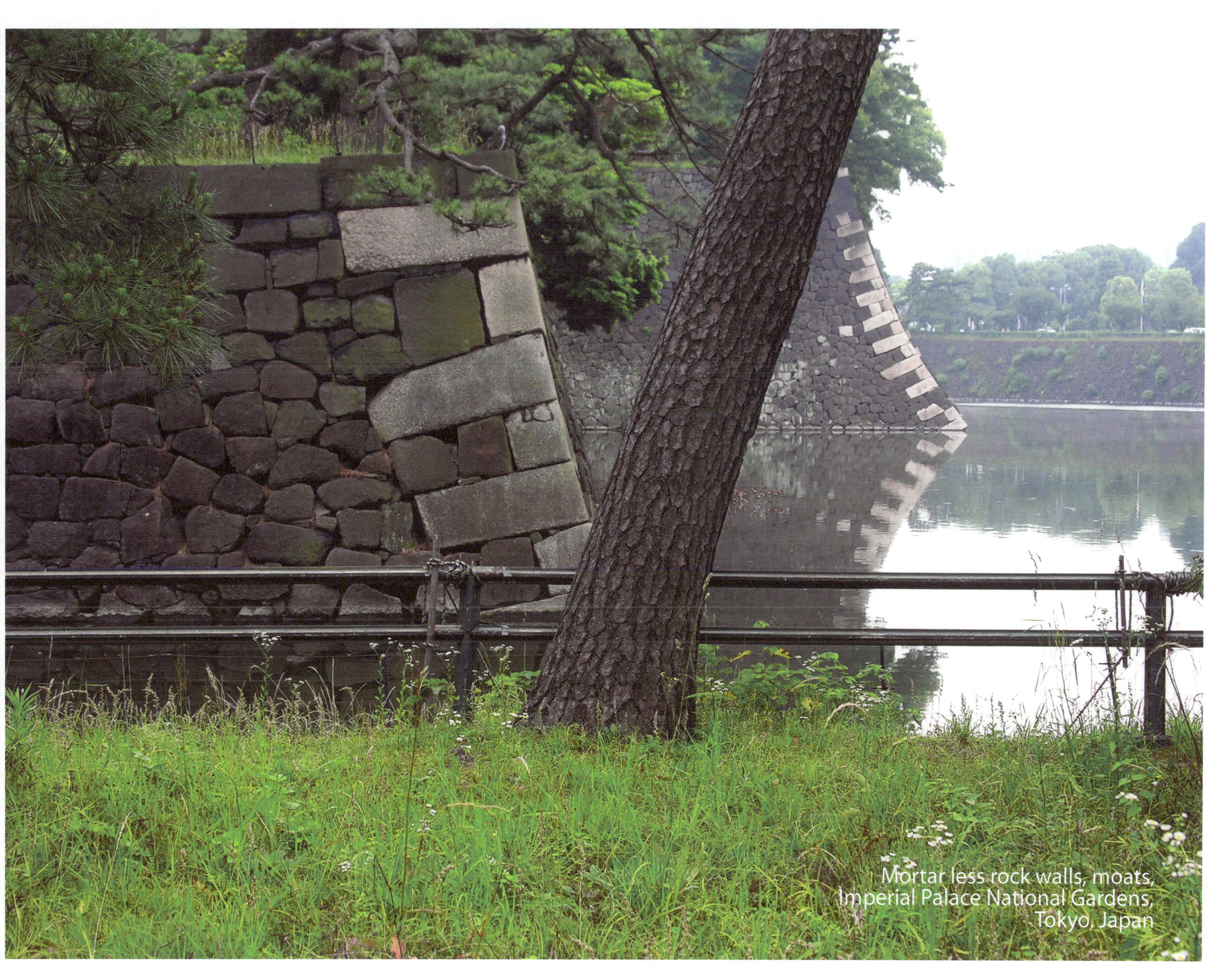

Mortar less rock walls, moats,
Imperial Palace National Gardens,
Tokyo, Japan

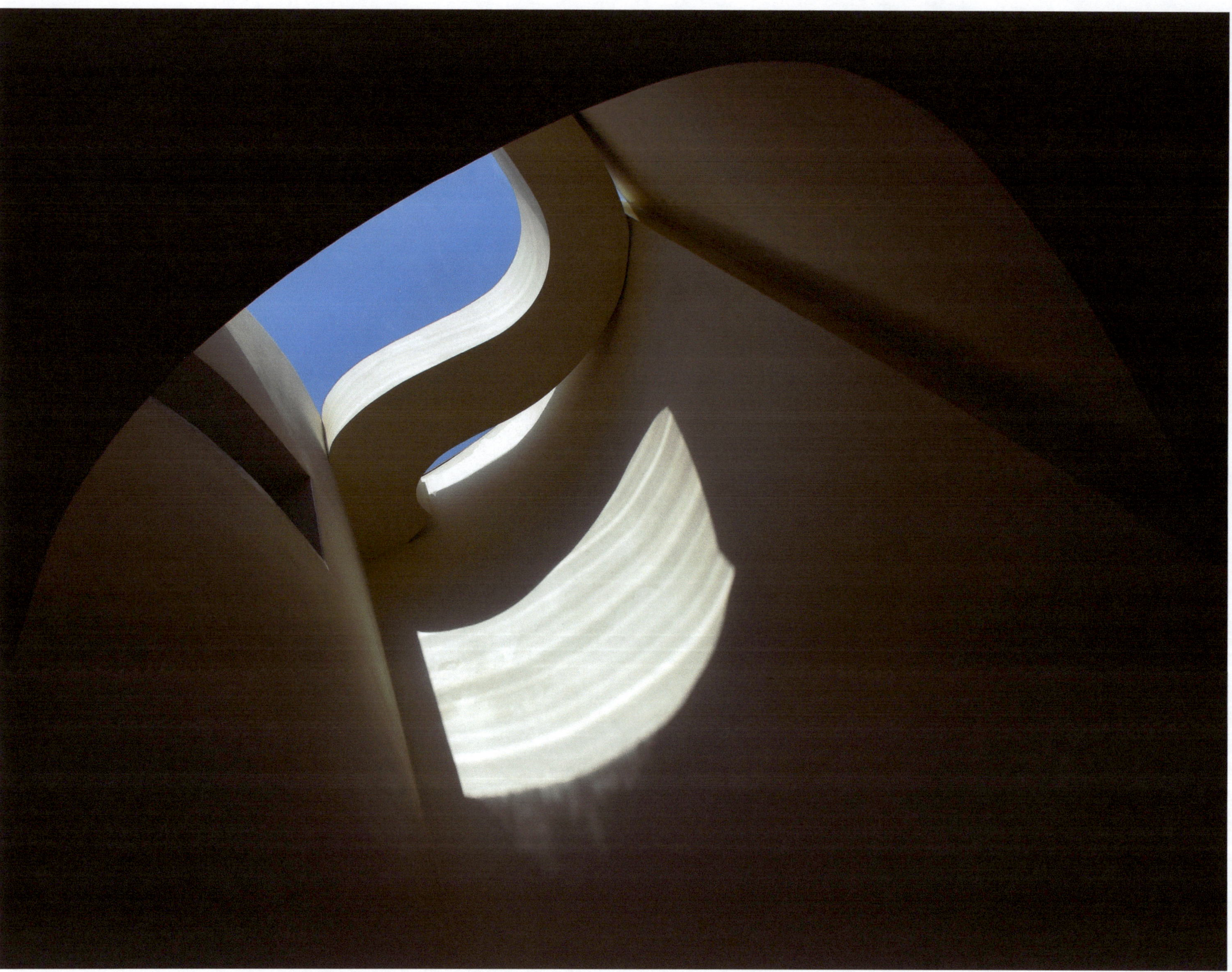

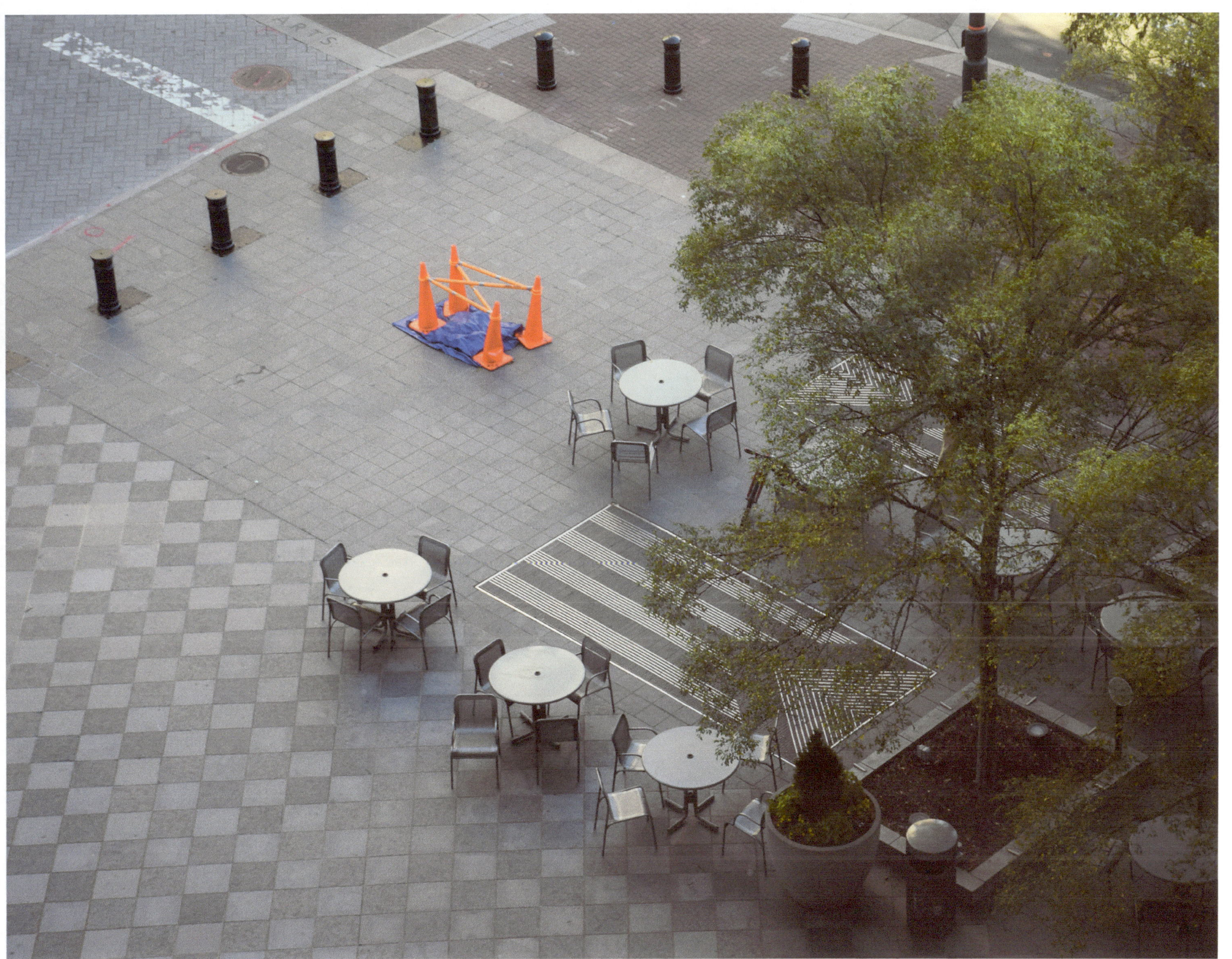

Climactic changes in the atmosphere, the fresh, cool colors of a new morning, the soothing quiet of falling snow, the pitter-patter of rain, the fiery sunsets of red, orange, and yellow against the deep blue sky, insist on photographically capturing that moment of awe to end your day. Equally insistent on photography are those times of terror, marked by dramatic hurricanes, tornadoes, lightning, thunder, drenching rain, floods, winds, and fires.

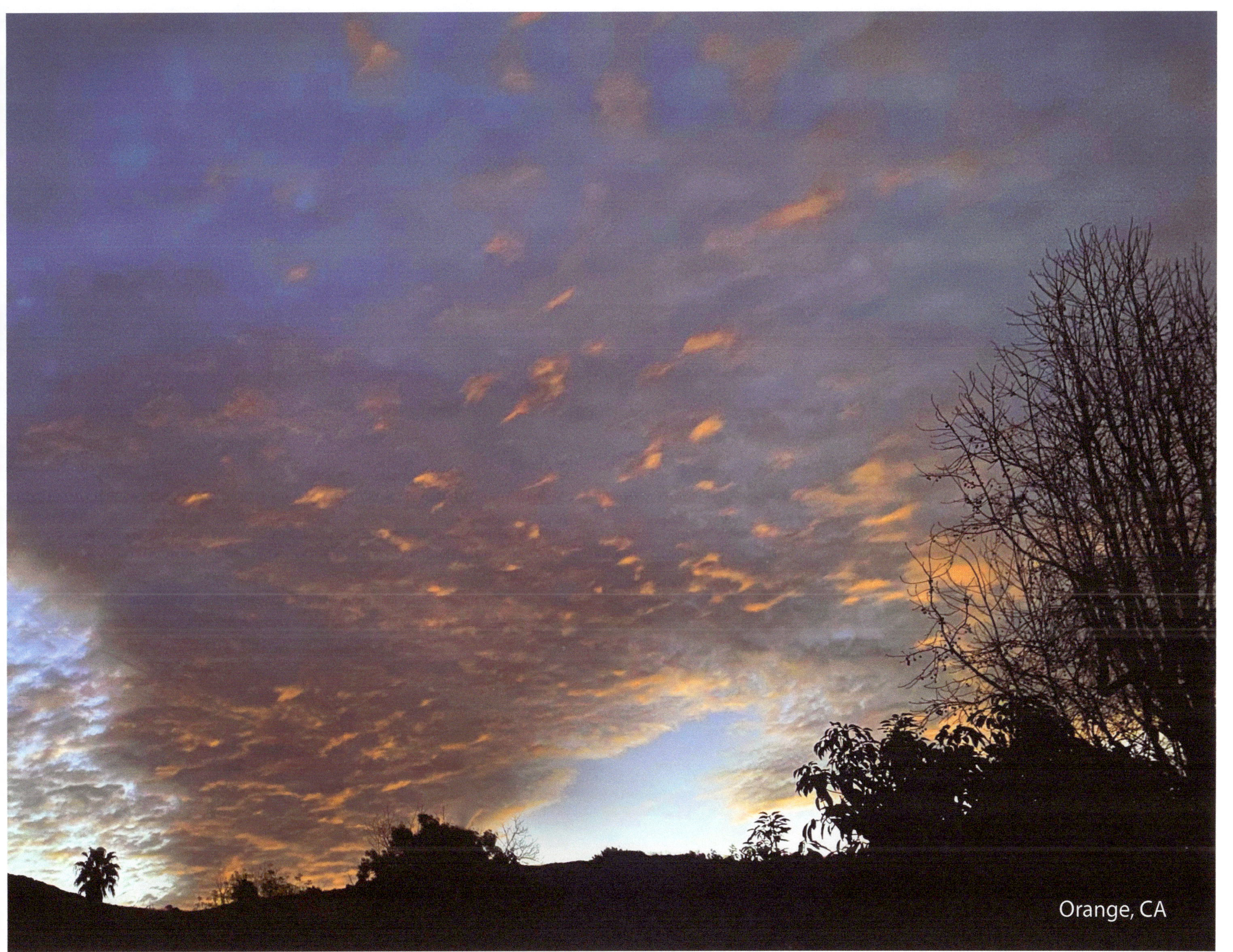
Orange, CA

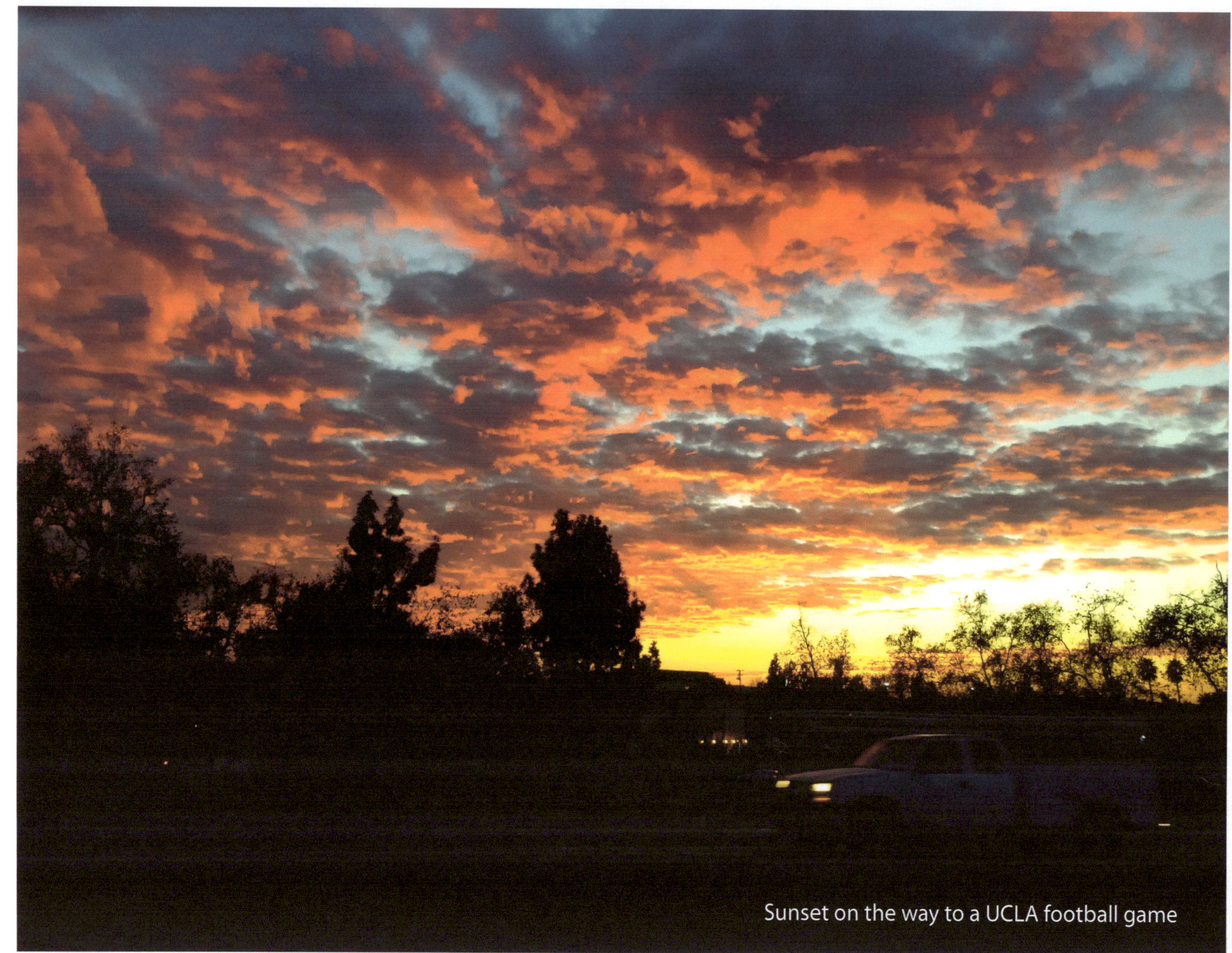
Sunset on the way to a UCLA football game

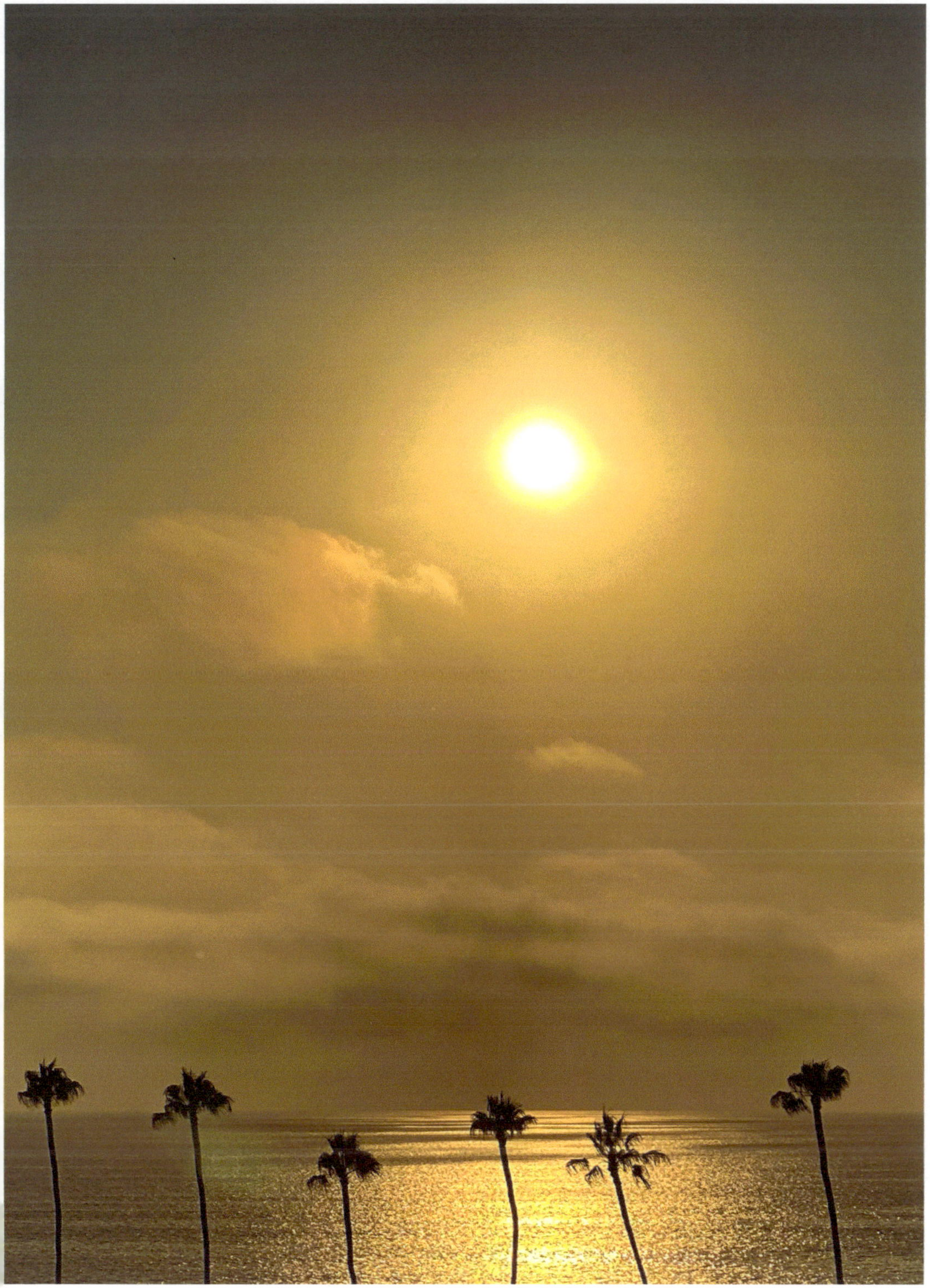

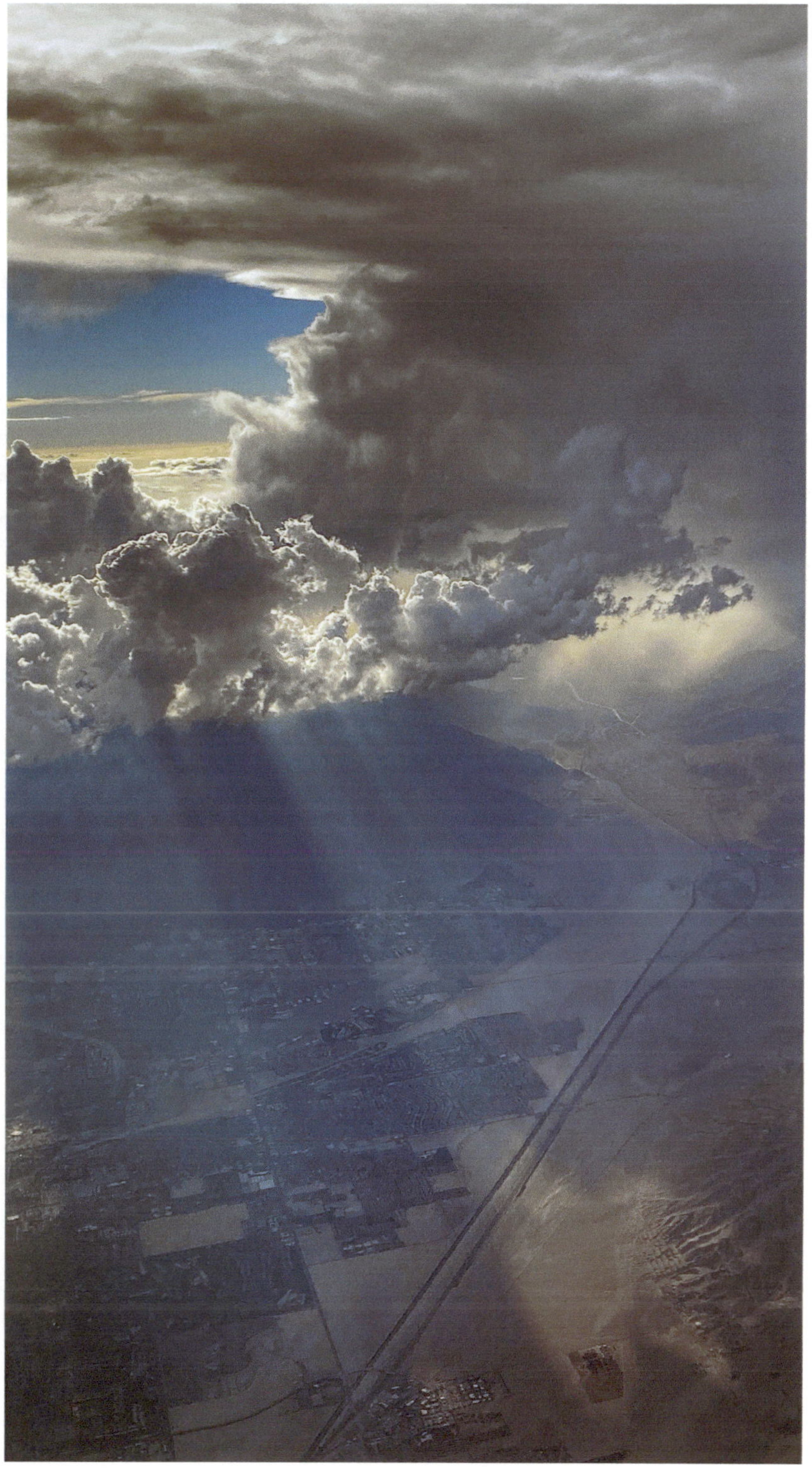

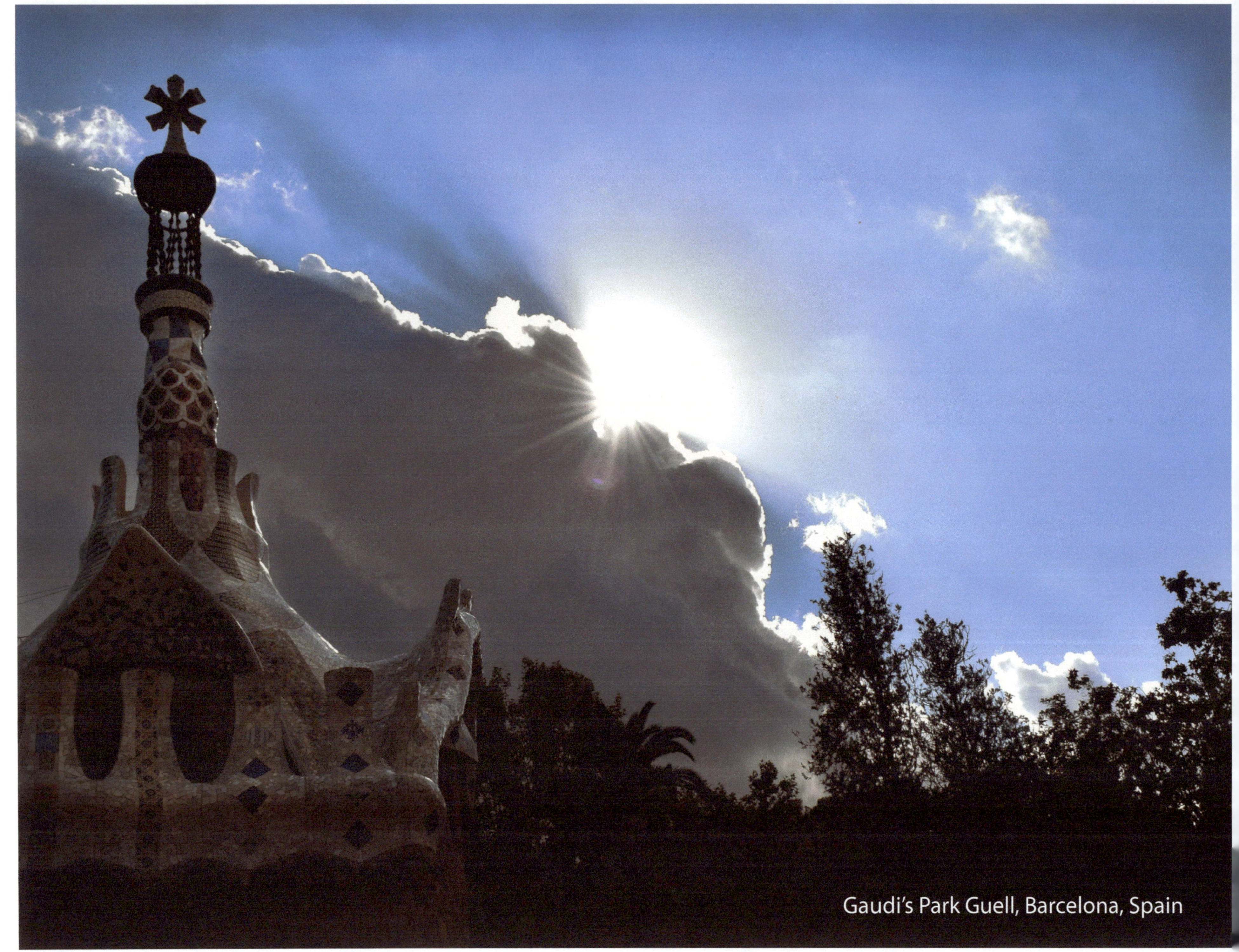

Gaudi's Park Guell, Barcelona, Spain

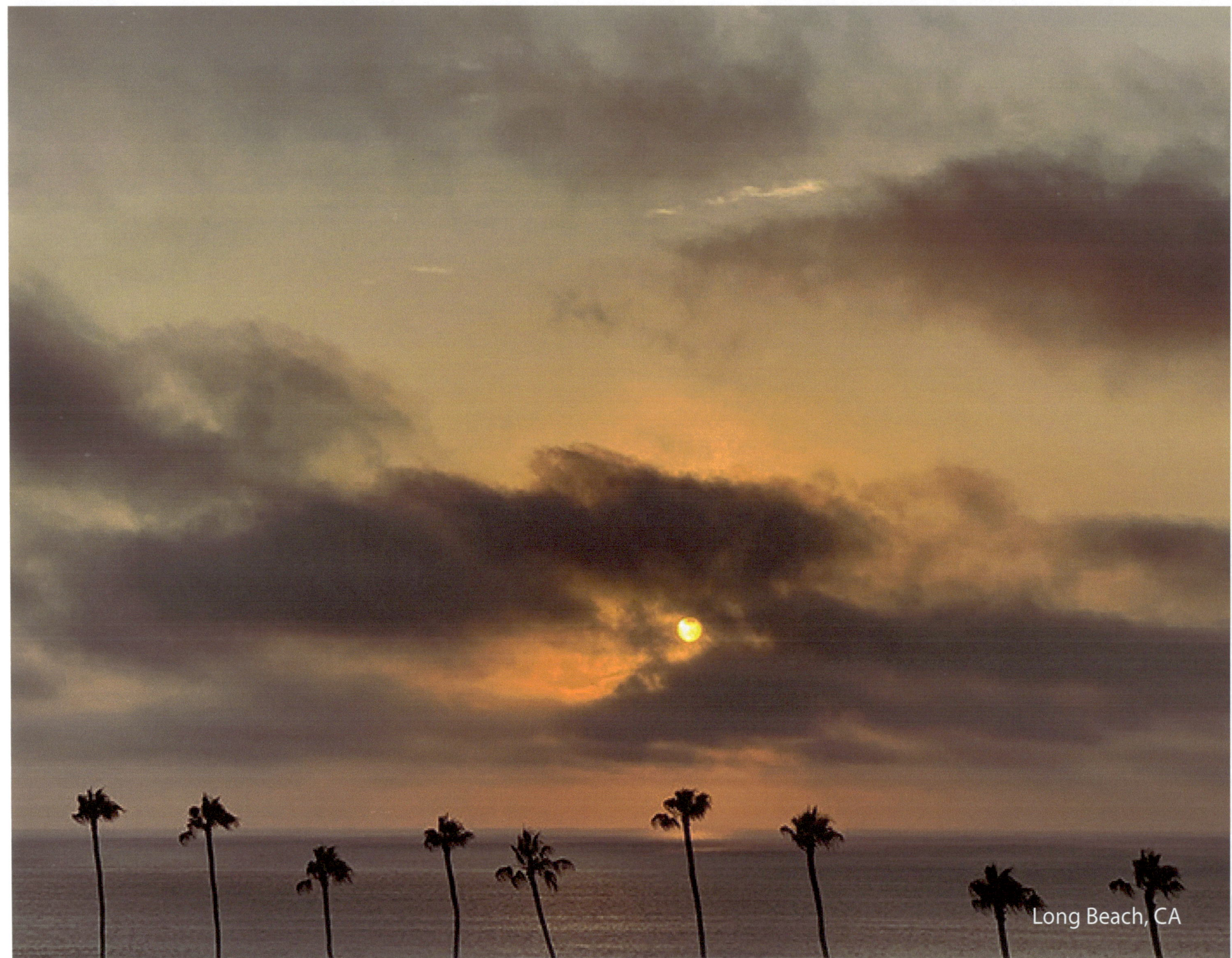
Long Beach, CA

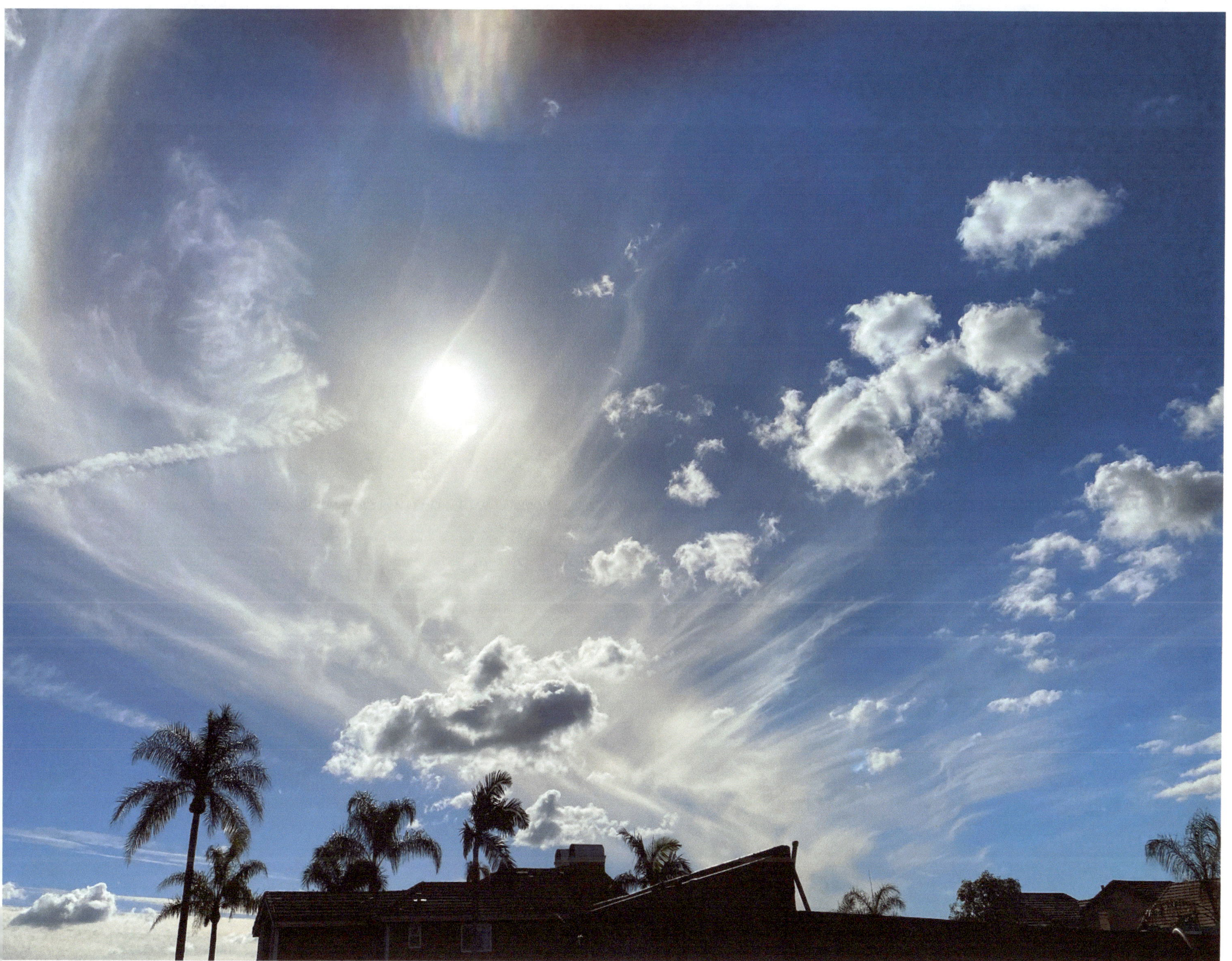

Then, of course, those odd, very personal images that are difficult
to categorize. They are only privy to the eye of the beholder – like
many observations – interesting to some and weird to others. But,
in the end, there are those moments in conversation when
someone flips through thousands of images on their cellphone,
trying to find a photo that illustrates a point they are to make.

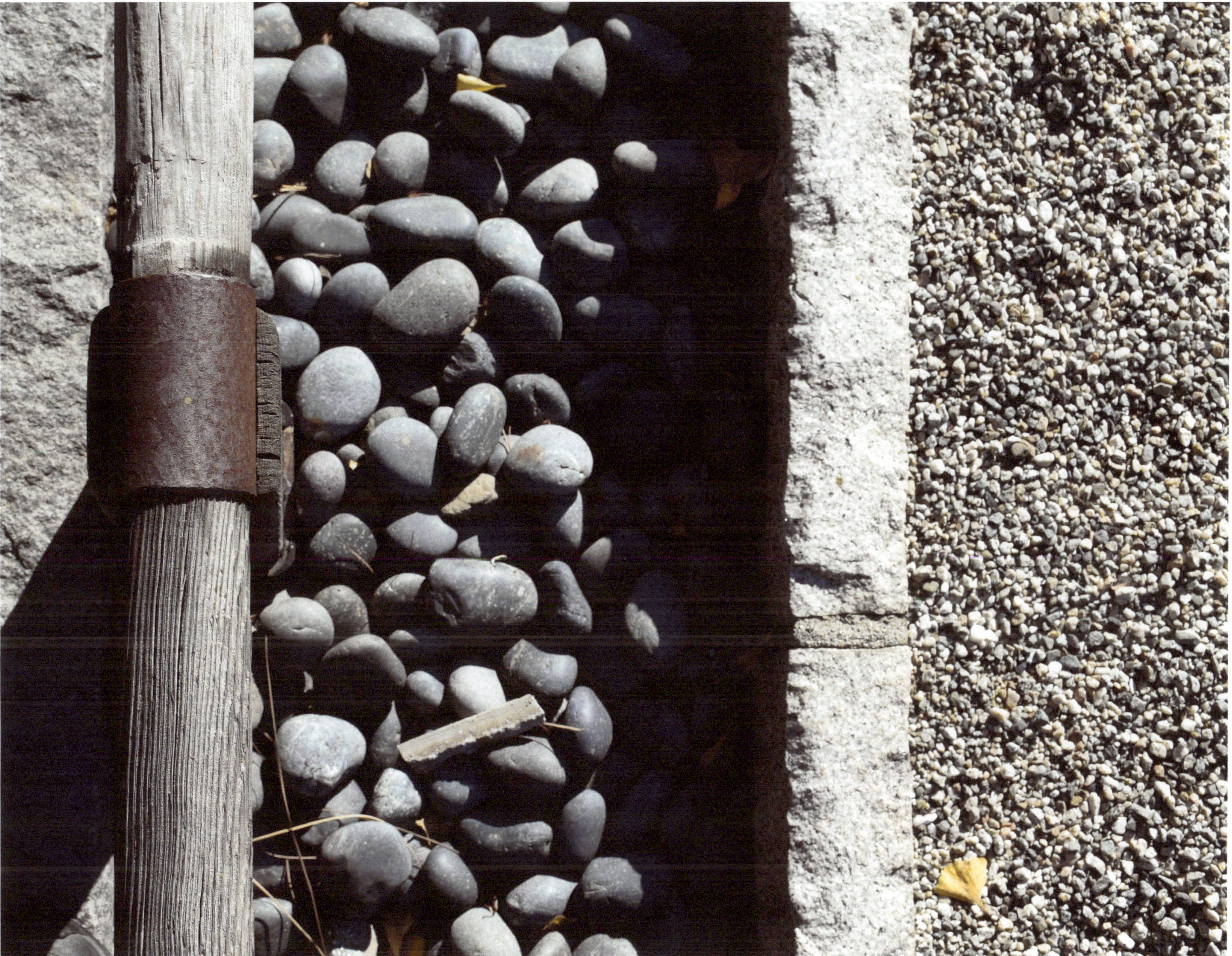

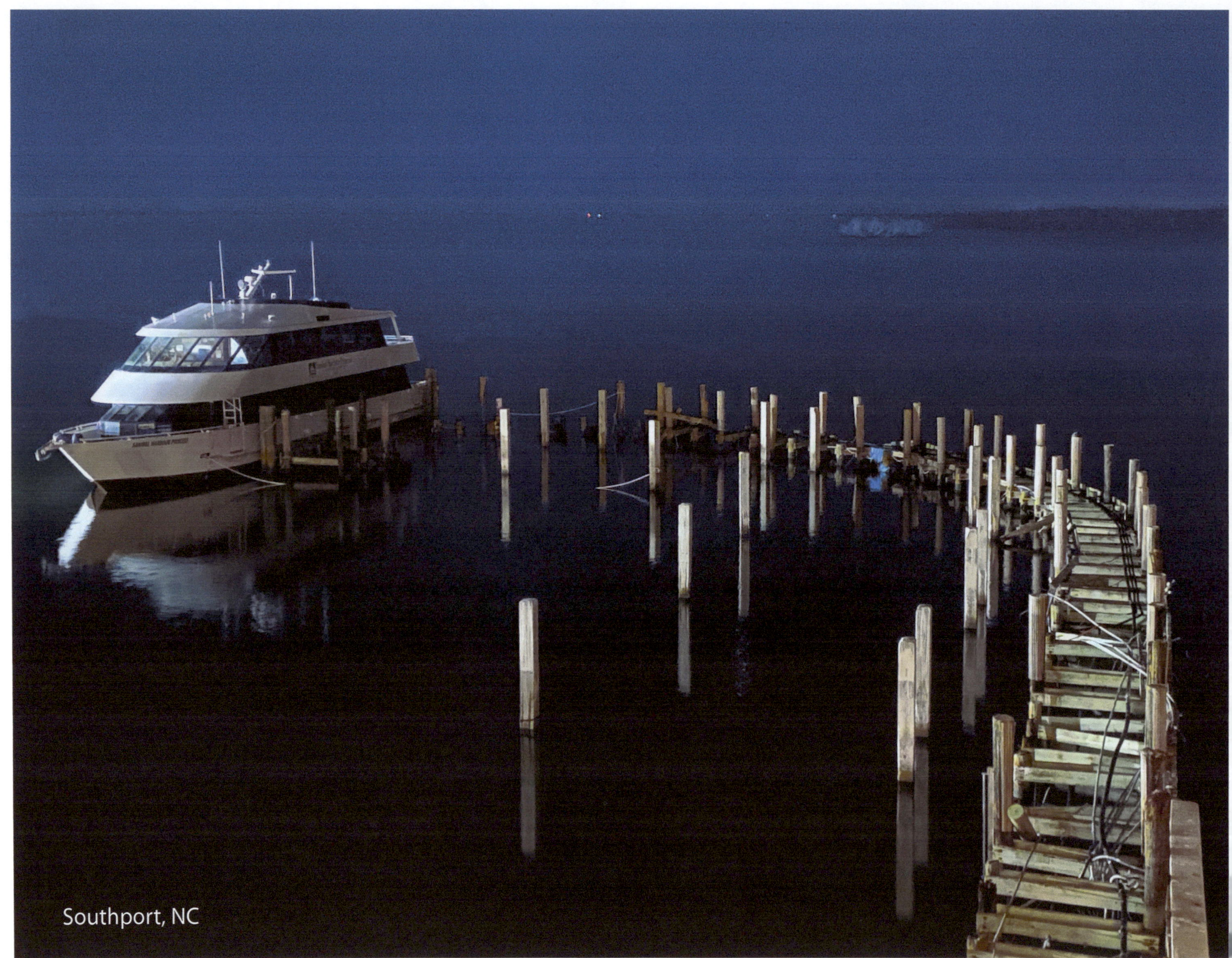

Southport, NC

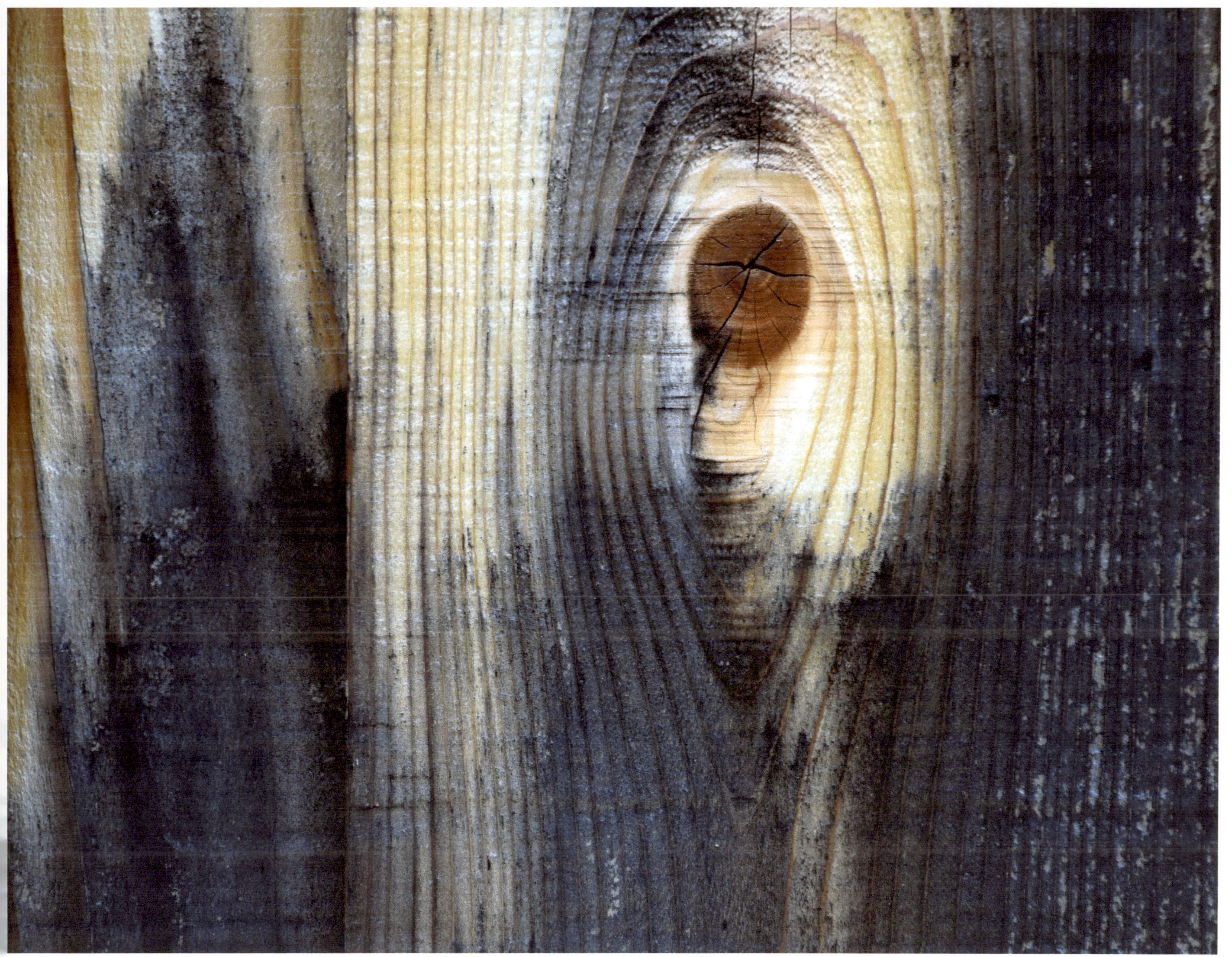

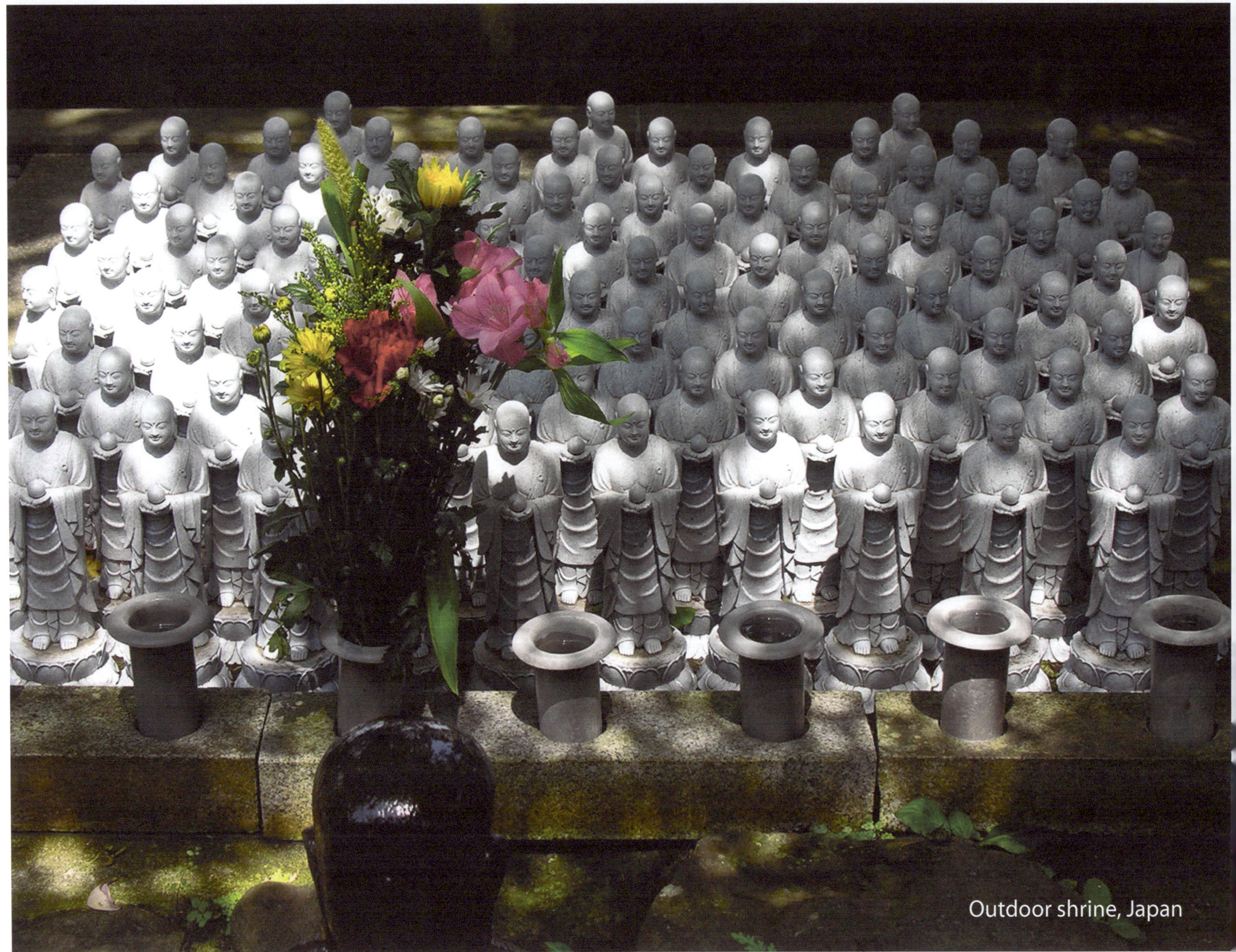

Outdoor shrine, Japan

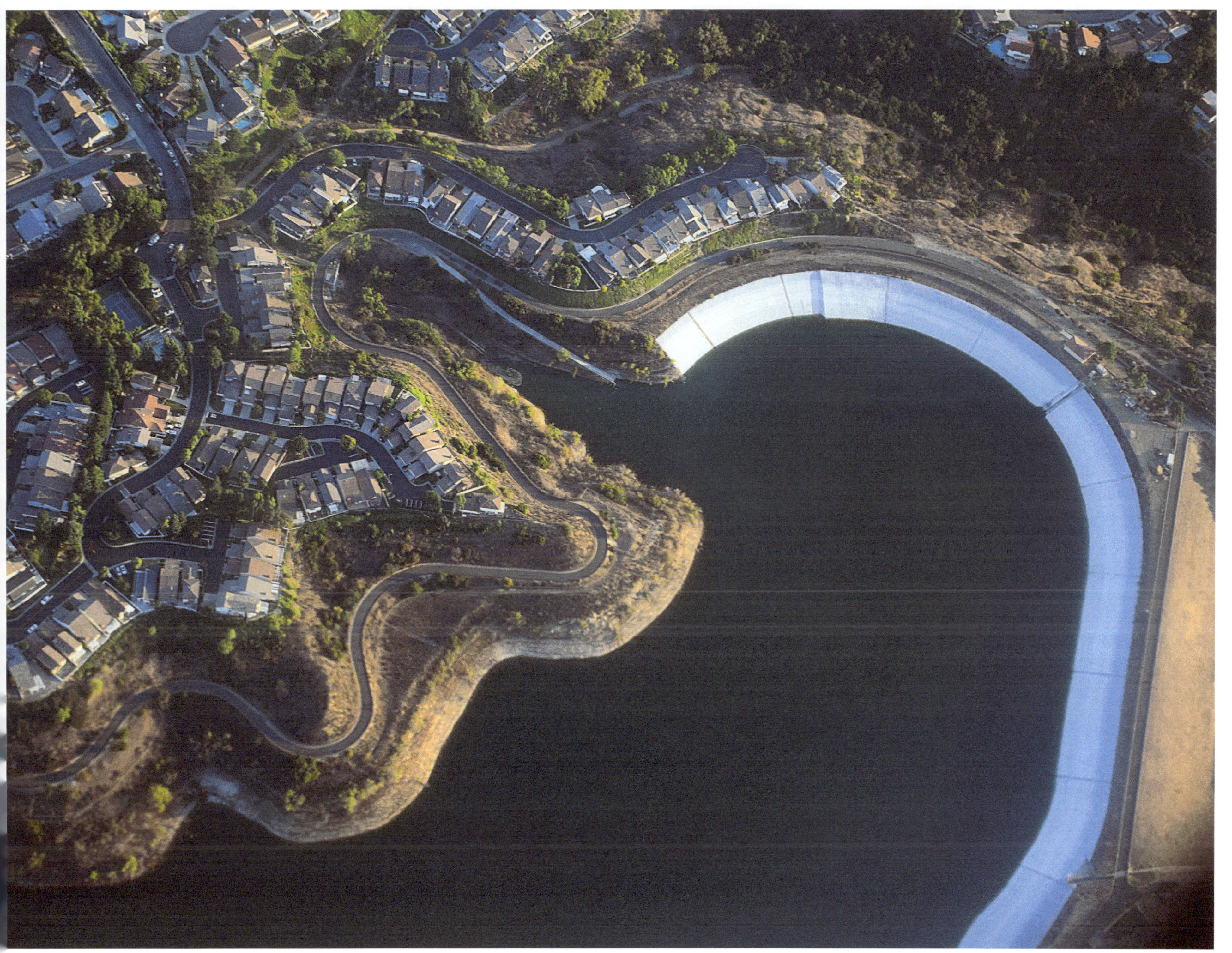

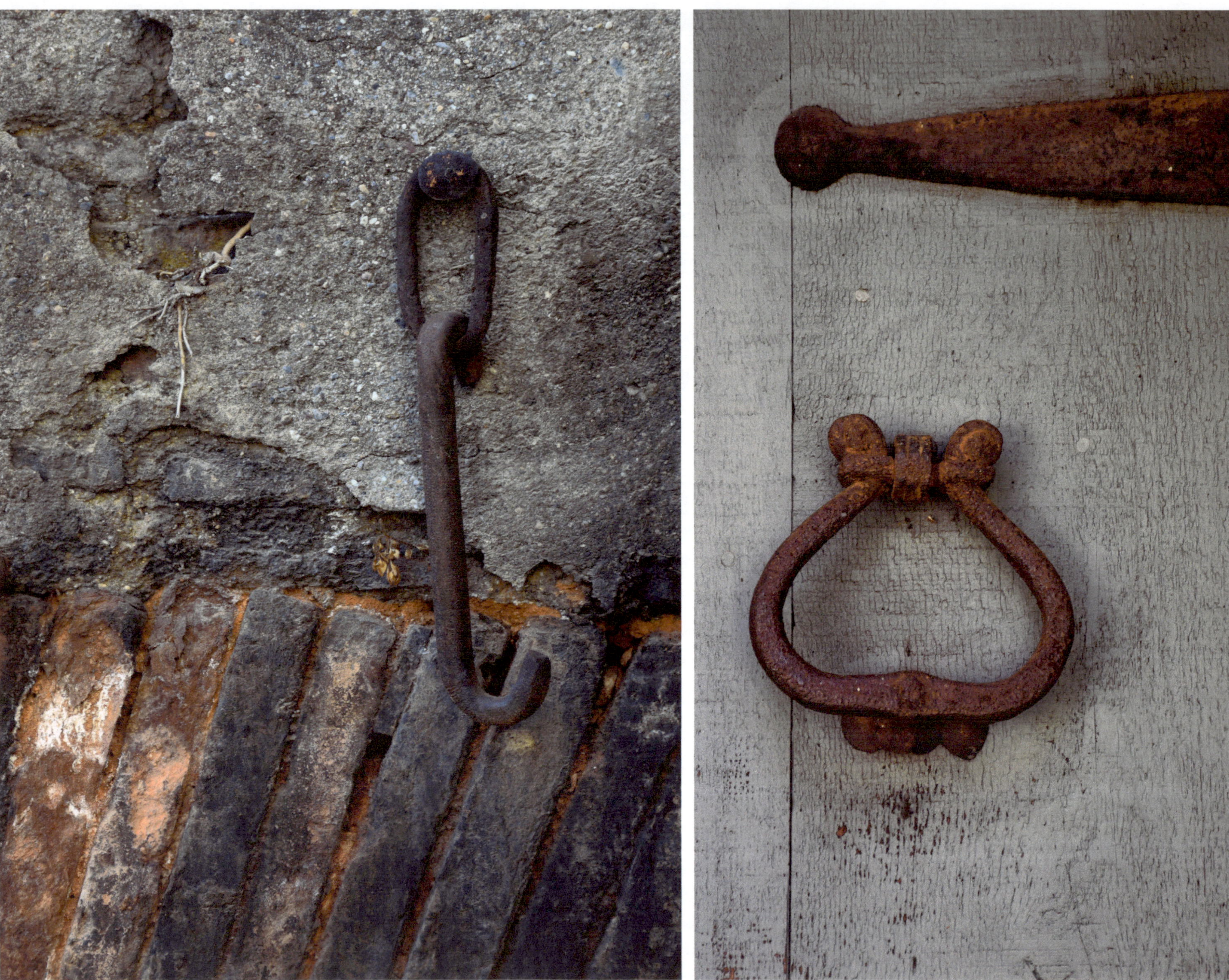

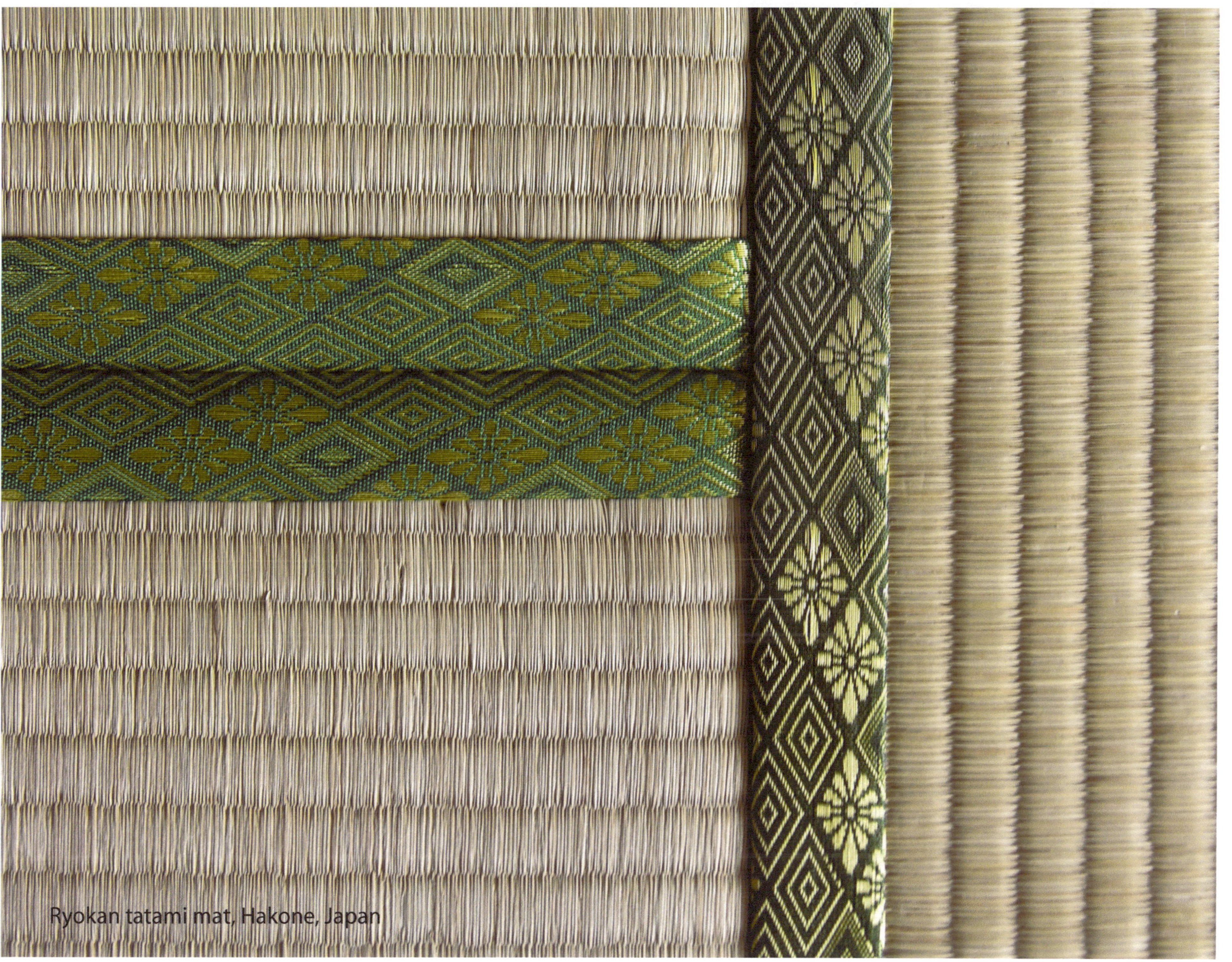

Ryokan tatami mat, Hakone, Japan

*There are always
two people in every picture:
the photographer and the viewer.*

- Ansel Adams

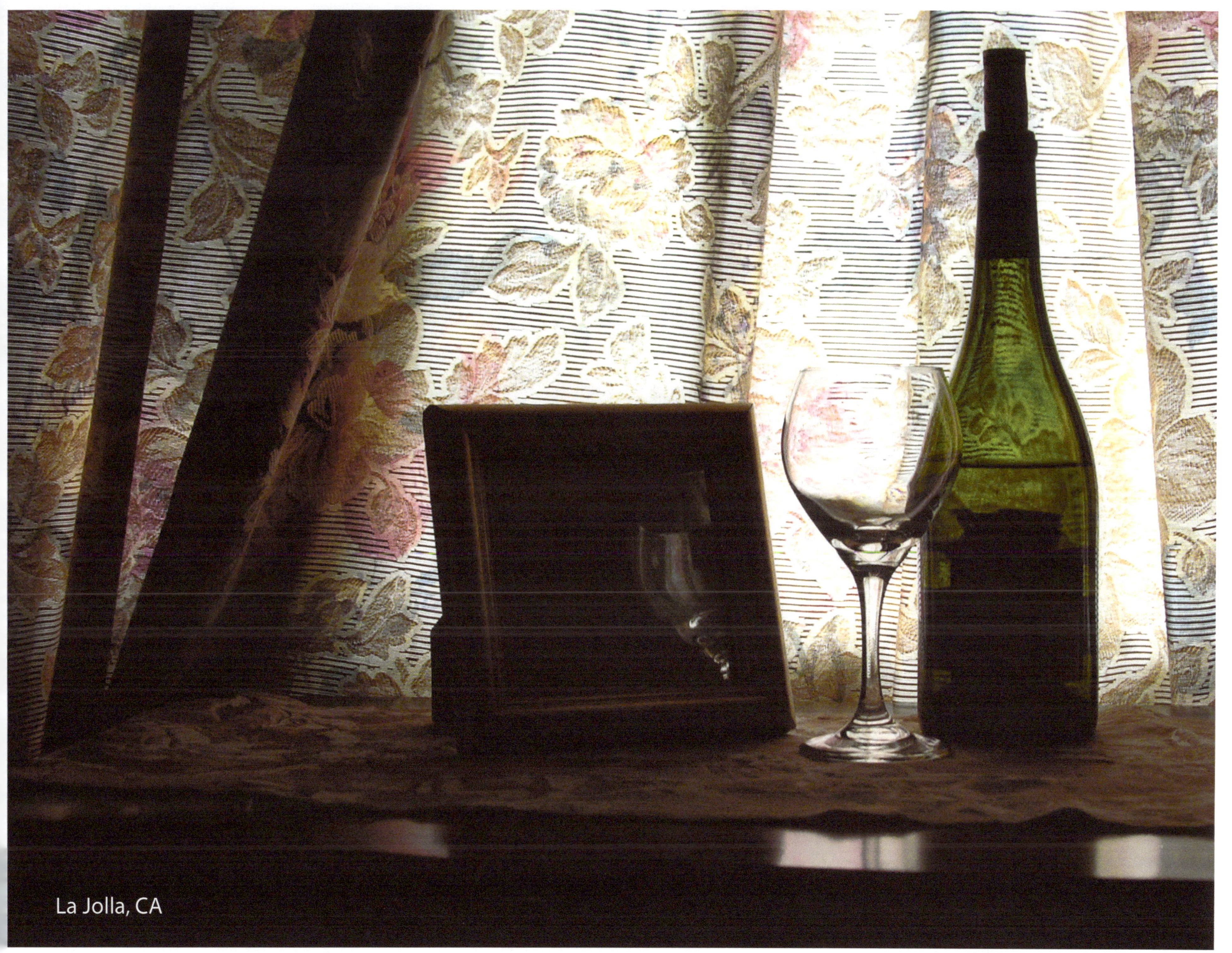
La Jolla, CA

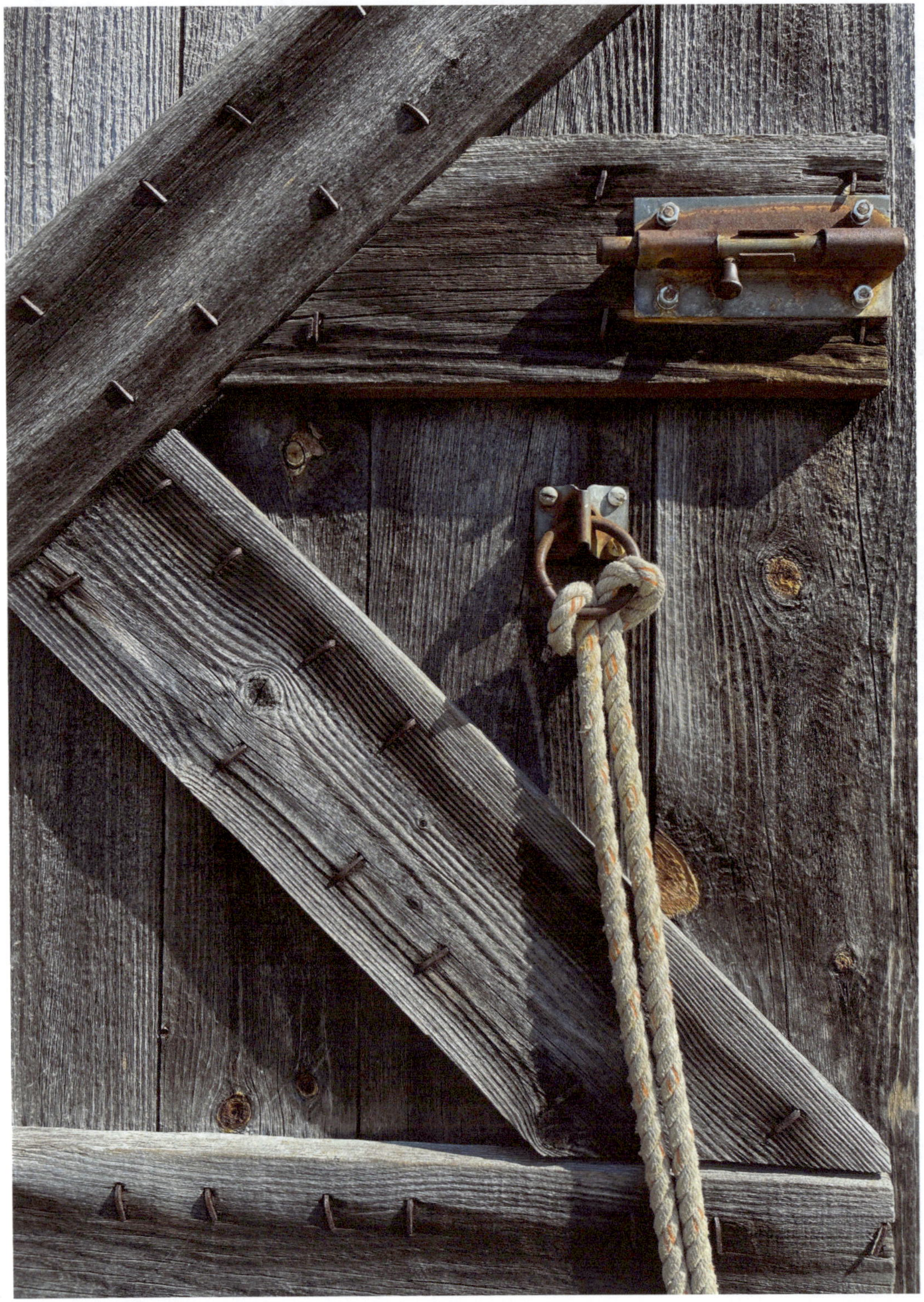

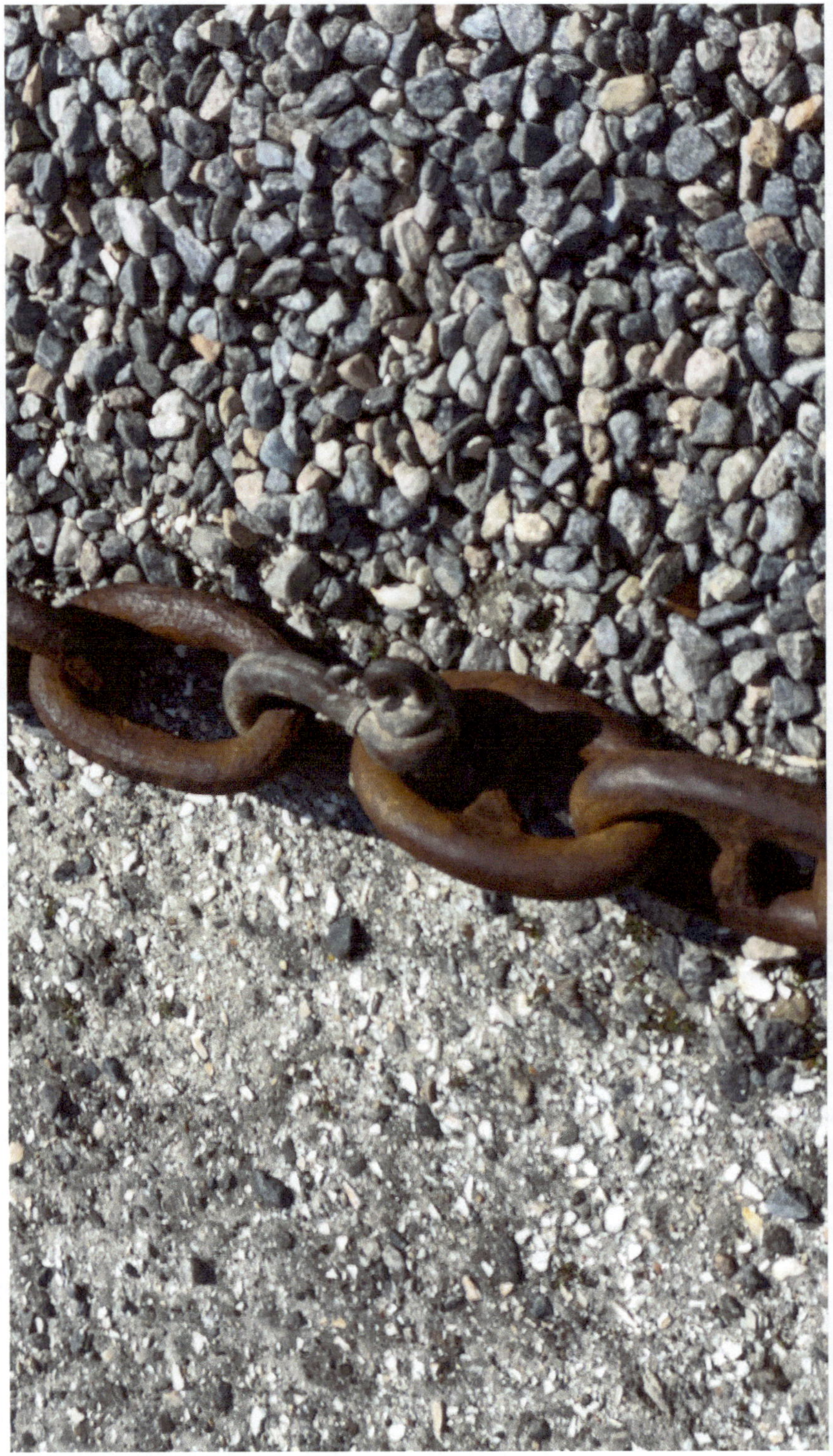

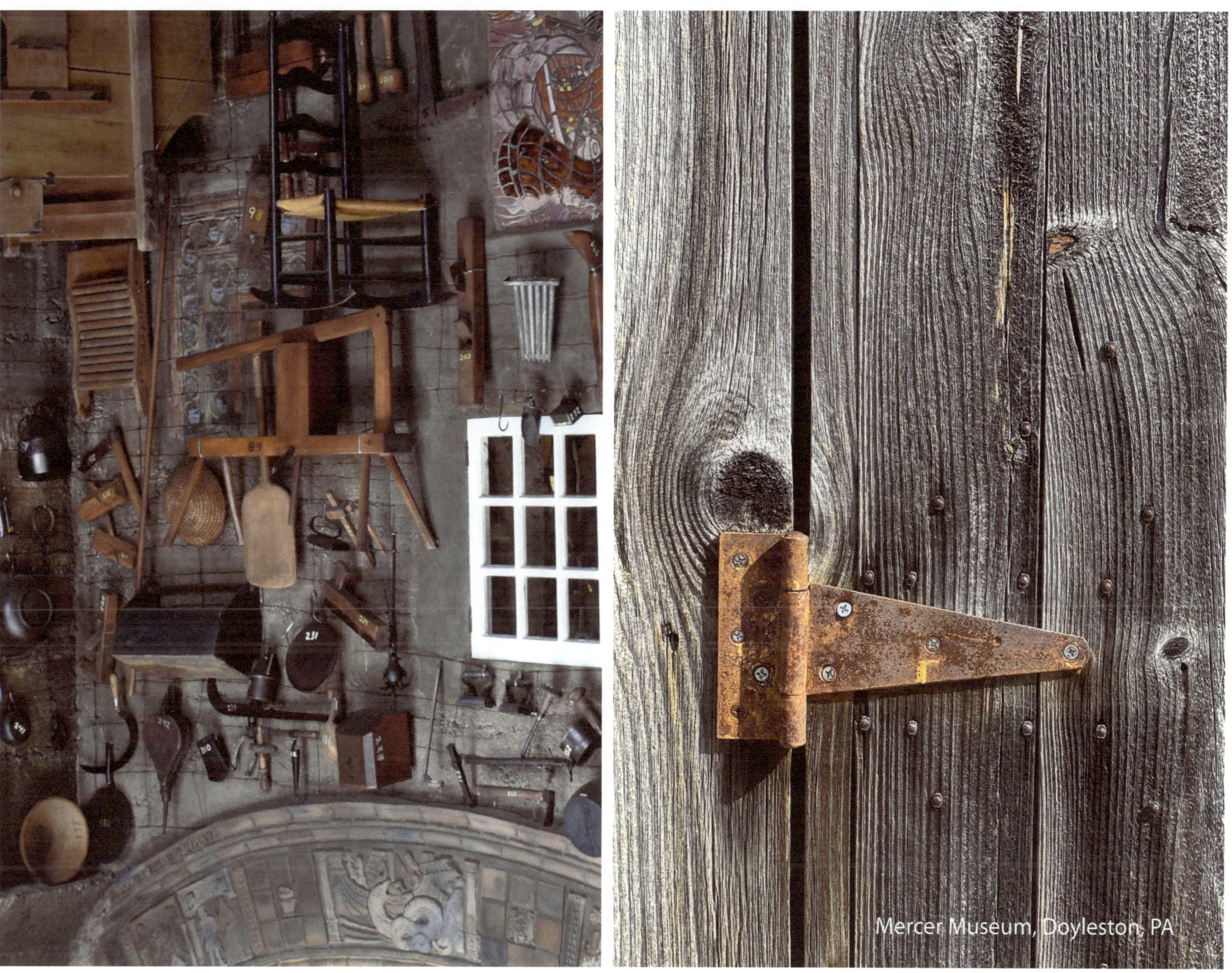
Mercer Museum, Doyleston, PA

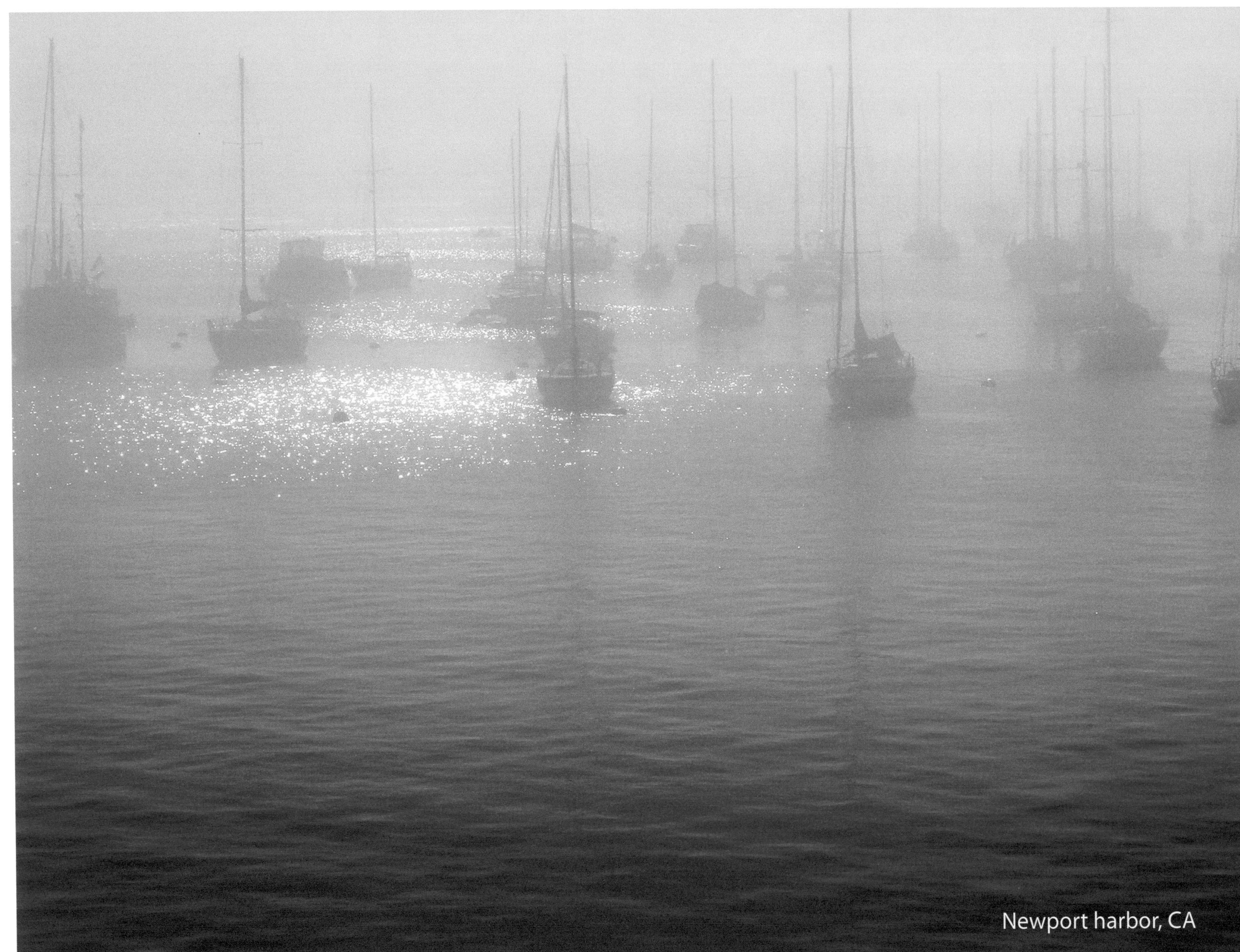
Newport harbor, CA